THE
POWER
METHOD

The ultimate guide for women who are ready to reclaim their strength, excel in leadership, and create work-life integration in the most powerful way.

BY: Sandra Haseley

The Power Method

The ultimate guide for women who are ready to reclaim their strength, excel In leadership, and create work-life integration in the most powerful way.

THE POWER METHOD

CHAPTER OUTLINE

INTRODUCTION

PART I – YOUR BUILT-IN POWER

CHAPTER 1 – WHAT THEY SAID ABOUT YOU

CHAPTER 2 – IT'S NOT A SCAR, IT'S GOLD

CHAPTER 3 - FROM PAIN TO POWER

CHAPTER 4 – FEEDBACK IN THE FAILURE

PART II - LEGEND-LIKE LEADERSHIP

CHAPTER 5 – SHE'S NOT A LEADER, SHE'S A *GIRL*!

INTRODUCTION

You've made it to adulthood. You're a capable human being. You're fairly reliable. Your cooking is aight. You're living in a nice home. You have family and friends who care about you. You're managing a lot. It looks like you're holding it together...

Then how are there still situations that make you feel like you're not doing enough? Or worse, that *you're* not enough?

How is it possible that for as much as you've done and as much as you can do, you don't feel energized or empowered by what you're doing?

This book is all about women, and ultimately their power, but not in a way that has anything to do with power over anyone else. And in case it needs to be said, feminine power isn't some soft, ethereal concept and it's not some light and fluffy idea to make us feel better about any of our weaknesses.

Quite the opposite. Women have the power to manage family and friends, juggle multiple high priority projects, create life, plan celebrations, earn a great living, speak up for change, influence governments, invent world-changing technologies, generate music and art that influences cultures forever, feel deeply, love hard, persevere, forgive, break down, and get back up again and again.

Despite the odds, women have a history steeped in power, strength, and leadership, while weaving together their work and personal life with what can seem like ease to those on the outside looking in.

I've had the honor of being surrounded by powerful women throughout my life. I was raised by them, played sports with them, learned from them, networked with them, and read about them.

And the more women I met, the more stories I heard. The experiences women have shared with me have rocked me to my core at times. Watching women, standing strong, with smiles, joy, and confidence dripping from them, while they tell a story of trauma, loss, sacrifice, pain, or injustice.

After a while, I felt like I was collecting these women's stories, in a sense, and borrowing this insane strength they had to somehow be okay on the other side of the incredibly challenging things they went through. Borrowing from their undeniable tenacity and determination to figure out a way to keep going, and as often as possible, find joy despite the pain.

There was a commonality among these powerful women and whether or not they knew they were doing it, they were all owning their power, leading in their own unique way, and managing life with so many more moving parts than just work and home.

If so many different personalities of women from so many different backgrounds and cultures all shared these similarities then that would have to mean these powerful methods are available to all of us.

I kept thinking to myself, *"What If women knew how to tap into their power; can you imagine what this world would look like?"*

I started featuring a handful of women from history during Women's History Month in March of 2021 on Facebook. I went live to tell their stories, but in a 2021 kinda way. I wanted to give voices to the women who either invented something incredible or took action that became responsible for creating the world as we know it today. Especially since nobody had ever seemed to have heard of them!

I called it *Every Day Miracle Women of History*, and their stories were like jet fuel for my own self-belief, turning into a catalyst for this book to finally come to life.

This book is written in honor of the women who:

- taught me lessons, especially the hard ones
- gave me advice that would end up saving my life
- volunteered to help in ways I've never seen anyone do when I thought a dark period might break me
- let me in their circle even though it seemed like I didn't belong
- serve our country and communities fearlessly while keeping us safe
- kept trying despite the fact that the deck had always seemed stacked against them
- showed me what it looked like to make scary choices and bet on myself, believing that I could go bigger

• and for the women of history who proved it only takes one good idea, dedication, and a little bit of guts to change the world, even if it seems like you have no resources at all

Oh but you thought this was JUST a book?!

Come 👏 on 👏 now–UHHH!

Sure, I could write a book, cross my fingers, and wish you "good luck", hoping it's enough. But the high-performance strategist in me says, "we can do better".

So instead, I'm delivering to you an experience with practical applications baked into The Power Method (apropos, don't ya think?), because while it's great to read things, feel good, and have a little extra "oomph" for a few days, it's WAY more powerful to actually DO something about it when you're already in motion.

I challenge you to actually *use* these tools as you advance through the pages.

Don't let the concepts in this book be another set of good ideas that sit on a shelf.

Let this book change your mind, open your heart, fill your confidence, and reboot your perception of worth by doing the work *while* you're reading. It's time to discover just how powerful you are.

Your power isn't a negative characteristic, nor is it something to fear.

Boasting about power is.

Fighting for power is.

But when we realize that power isn't something we have to fight for, it's something we've had along, then it's just a matter of digging it up within us, reigniting it, and letting it be the fuel that allows us to lead ourselves and lead others.

Get ready to #GOBIGGER.

PART I | YOUR BUILT-IN POWER

pow·er
/ˈpou(ə)r/

1. *the ability to do something or act in a particular way, especially as a faculty or quality.*
2. *a person or organization that is strong or influential within a particular context.*
3. *a supernatural being, deity, or force.*
4. *the capacity or ability to direct or influence the behavior of others or the course of events.*

According to the Oxford Languages, these are just some of the definitions of power.

You wanna know where it started though?

The word, "power" comes from the Anglo-Normal French word, "poeir", which was altered from the original Latin, "posse", meaning *"be able"*, or *"can"*.

Hmmmm... "Can." When we have power, that essentially means we *can*.

If *any* word could be a synonym for "woman", *can* can.

Just like all women, you were born with all the right parts on the inside. You've been given gifts, abilities, and intuition that have been baked into you like computer coding. It's more common than ever, due to life's ever-increasing distractions, that women are forgetting what that really means.

If someone were able to go through your entire life, from birth 'til now, and list out all the ways you've shown up as a powerful girl or woman, you wouldn't be able to question it. But those examples are probably dormant for you, lying somewhere deep in the back of your memory, rarely if ever, accessed again.

But what if you could start collecting those examples? What if you could start recognizing ways you really *are* powerful? Instances where you've felt like you could do anything if you were able to accomplish whatever it was that you just did.

You can. And my aim in this part of the book is to help you see how much power you've had all along, and to view yourself in a way that makes you feel so capable to take on any next big goal you have.

Let's get into and for cryin' out loud, let's #GOBIGGER!

CHAPTER 1

WHAT THEY SAID ABOUT YOU

I went to grab my lunch off the counter that my mom had packed and she'd just walked into the kitchen. She asked, *"You all set for your presentation?"*, and my stomach dropped a little but I said, "I think I'm ready. I practiced a lot but I'm still a little nervous.".

"Don't be nervous, be excited instead. You know this stuff well and besides, all the kids in the class have to give their presentation at some point too, so just do your best because no one's there to judge you. They're all just trying to get through it."

I took a deep breath at that because she was right. No one wanted to give a presentation on a random historical person whom we didn't even get to choose for ourselves. My classmates were probably more worried about how *they* would perform when it was their turn, rather than how well I would do while I was presenting. The thing she said next dropped me right back into panic mode.

"Just remember to SLOOOOOW DOOOOOWN!".

This wasn't the first time I'd heard this. I was a junior in high school at the time so I'd done, what, a couple of dozen presentations in front of a classroom by now? My mom started warning me about the speed of my speech in high school. Worried that my nerves would allow me to shift into warp speed in order to get the public speaking tragedy over with as quickly as possible. In which case, I might get a lower mark since I'd be speaking at a pace no one could follow.

Out of complete fairness, let me be clear. My mom has always been a champion for me and each of my 3 siblings. She knows us well and understands our weaknesses and strengths, doing what she can to encourage and support us so that we'll feel empowered and capable. She's a good mom, Nope. She's a fantastic mom.

But I often *did* speak quickly. Not only when I was nervous, but also when I was excited, happy, angry, or focused. So as any of those emotions increased, so too did the words flying out of my mouth. It was because my mom believed in me that she wanted me to stand up in front of my teacher and peers with a sense of control and power in order to keep a room captive. I just didn't realize that at the time.

I was warned before presentations not only by my mother but by my teachers as well. I was always speaking nearly as fast as the thoughts came into my head, more like a stream of consciousness than anything else. So the teachers who liked me would frequently say things like, *"remember to take a deep breath before you start and slooooooooow dowwwwwwwwwn"*.

Once I graduated high school and later, university, I was so relieved that I wouldn't have to deal with any speech-speed warnings again. But I quickly found out, early in my career, that grown-ups don't have a problem sharing their unsolicited opinions with other grown-ups. So I started hearing, "slow down" from coworkers before sales meetings or conference calls, to make sure the others in the room could keep up with me.

Based on how the recommendations were delivered, they made me feel diminished, incapable, and childish because children are the ones who need to be told to slow down. In fact, children are the *only* ones that are supposed to get instructions on how to "human" from grown-ups, aren't they?

None of the people who'd ever advised me to keep a slower pace during speaking engagements meant to make me feel small, I know that now. But at the time, when peers on the same level or rank as me would give me those recommendations, it made me feel as though I didn't belong and something was wrong with me. No one else was getting that advice.

I graduated with an impressive degree, I was always a high achiever, yet I had to be reigned in periodically by others despite the levels I'd climbed in life, and it made me question my intelligence, my ability to communicate with others, and my ability to succeed. It began to shape the way I saw myself. It created a new level of insecurity for me that made me turn down opportunities based on a developed lack of confidence in my competence to execute on the most basic of human interactions.

So rather than accepting a great job offer, I made excuses for why I might not be a good fit for an interview. Instead of meeting with a new prospect that was introduced, sometimes I passed them off to someone I thought might be more proficient. The kind of opportunities that would have set me on a much more successful trajectory than what ended up occurring for me then.

In the end, my mother, the teachers, and some of my colleagues were right based on best practices in society. They'd given me advice that was preparing me for a world where I'd need to conform to a set of rules and expectations. Succeeding in a classroom, followed by a boardroom, perhaps a podium, a sales meeting, or a group of investors, meant that I'd need to present a certain way to be taken seriously.

What was uncommon at the time, was to imagine that a child might grow up and do life differently than the traditional education system and corporate culture had groomed them for. Because the safer bet seemed to be the highway where the rest of the world was going.

They weren't thinking about the beautiful trail off the main drag, and how that trail might just take me out in the world to create something incredible of my own, and speak in my own way so that my tribe, my people, would hear it, see it, and recognize their people. That maybe this child was never meant for conforming and doing things the average way. Maybe that child was never average and felt squeezed and uncomfortable with everyone else who was willing to settle.

Over time we become conditioned through experiences, circumstances, and relationships in a way that shows our cracks and vulnerabilities. Then, when things go wrong as a result of those imperfections, the world around us tells us it's because we're deficient in those areas. Because hey, we're clearly struggling in ways the majority of people might not be. And little by little we can allow the stories and memories of those imperfections, those let-downs, disappointments, and perceived failures, tell us that the message of our weakness is just a little bit louder than any of our greatness.

Let's time warp to the present, where I'm a mother of four incredible children, a founder of several successful companies, with a litany of magnificent experiences that created the woman I am today. I look back at my past with love and compassion, remembering the voices that told me I spoke too fast, moved too fast, that I was also too loud, too energetic, too sensitive, too rambunctious, and those words don't affect me anymore. I've found power in it. But when who you are, fundamentally, challenges someone else's perception of their own strengths, it's common for them to try to encourage you to conform.

I found out later that my "too muchness" was what so many people in the world resonated with and felt at home with, because they were "too much", too. I just hadn't met them yet because my social environment wasn't big enough to have access to all those beautiful souls across the world.

For the people that complained I spoke too loudly...

They simply didn't share the vigor I had for life, nor did they understand how passion has a way of increasing the volume of a conversation and that it might even inspire others by accident. They also couldn't realize that the act of projecting my voice became critical in my career, surrounded by a sea of old men in boardrooms and conference calls, in order for my opinions, perspectives, and ideas to be heard.

When the people around me criticized me for speaking too fast...

They weren't aware of how impossible it can be for so many of us to pay attention to someone who draws out their speech slowly and takes their sweet old time getting to the point. What they *never* seem to know, which I found out later from Ralph G. Nichols listening research, is that the human ear can hear at least two times faster than I could ever speak(hence the 2x and 4x speed options on communication apps like Voxer so I *know* I don't need to slow down.

For the people who told me I had too much energy...

They underestimated how much energy it actually takes to juggle 24 credit hours, Division 1 softball, and a part-time job. Which later turned into four kids, four different schools, health challenges, several businesses, traveling for work, COVID, and growing a team. Without the energy that I naturally have, which I view as a gift from God, none of those things would have been possible for me to handle with the same amount of success.

Oh, and the ones that thought I laughed too hard...

They're still trying to figure out how to find joy despite their circumstances. And I know now that it wasn't my big laughter that was so offensive to them. It was the joy they saw in my laugh that shone a spotlight on their own unhappiness, which made them uncomfortable with their ability to enjoy the moment or find the good in a bad situation.

And you might have heard some of those things too, or maybe the things you heard were different. Maybe you were too slow, or too quiet, too confusing, or too mysterious. Too artsy, too conservative, too liberal, too anything.

But if you let those small voices, from small-minded people that don't know any better, define what you're capable of, you've just handed over your power to people that never even realized they could take it.

There are typically a handful of traits about ourselves that people focus on. We all have a collection of strengths or differences that are perceived by others as abnormal. So one of the ways I've found helpful is to be prepared for the types of comments you'd rather not receive and be prepared with a power-response along with a more powerful reframe for it. Your chosen power-response allows you to take control in the moment, and the reframe you choose prevents their words from lingering and taking root so these hurtful things don't ever have to define you.

An example of the reframe can look like this:

Someone tells you you're too loud.

Your power response options are:

"I might be too loud for YOU, but this is the volume that feels great for me so I'm keeping it."

"You think I'm too loud but I don't think you're loud enough (with a confident, but understated smile)."

"Hmmm.. that's an interesting angle. My friends have never thought so, it's one of the things so many people love about me."

Your powerful reframe = You own your volume and you don't let their comment shame you, instead you shine a light on the confidence you have in how you operate in life, which is nothing less than inspiring to anyone witnessing the exchange.

Someone tells you you're too much.

Your power response options are:

"Too much is actually the perfect amount."

"I'm probably too much for you and if it bothers you I won't be offended in the least if you find other company."

"Am I? Or is it that you're just not enough?"

Your powerful reframe = People's opinions on what's too much is simply that. It's a perspective. The great thing about you being too much for other people is that it so quickly identifies who should and shouldn't be allowed in your space. And that can save a ton of time in life as you try to sift the "real ones" in your network, just as long as you're willing to own your too-muchness.

Someone tells you you're too slow.

Your power response options are:

"Maybe you're just going too fast."

"My pace always serves me so well in catching mistakes, making the best decisions, and finding out who has the kind of patience I like in a person."

"What a strange opinion." (often well-executed coupled with an expression of confusion at this person's comment, as though no one in the world would even agree with it...then simply carry on)

Your powerful reframe = You take their comment and flip it to support who you are and make them think about their uninvited judgment of you. You also let them know you're in control of who comes into your circle to stay and politely(with an edge) communicates that their unsolicited opinion has fallen into unwelcome territory.

Someone tells you you're too sensitive.

Your power response options:

"I feel deeply which allows me to connect deeply with people I love. I'm not too sensitive, I'm just very aware."

"I always feel bad for people who don't know how to feel (or empathize) in ways that I can, I can't imagine how isolating that must be. There's so much richness to experience and I'm so grateful for the gift of sensitivity."

"My ability to be sensitive to others has allowed me to catch critical non-verbal communications that other people have missed in my personal life, in business, in everything. I wouldn't trade this superpower for anything."

Your powerful reframe = You capsize their opinion of being "sensitive" by showing pride and ownership of how connected sensitive people are. Allowing them to see the power in it, especially since many people associate sensitivity with weakness when it's such an incredible strength.

People so often say things they don't mean, and many lack the emotional intelligence to appreciate the weight of their unwelcome words. So they react and can speak from a place so disconnected that they're completely unaware of the damage they might be doing.

And since you have no way of controlling everyone around you, the power-response and powerful reframe can help you gain the strength and practice to own your power.

Another way you can fortify yourself is by choosing to collect compliments from others that you get along the way. The kind of compliments you get that not only make you feel good but that you know are true (and ditch the humility for a second and just appreciate those strengths, you get to own those along with all of your other incredible attributes).

If you're visual like me, it might help you to imagine each compliment as a scale on a suit of armor. Starting off with the compliments you can remember from people, you can metaphorically build this suit of armor around you, adding to it another scale for every new compliment you receive. Imagine this armor being draped around you so that any negative comment you receive has no place to land on you. The negative can't take root when it's bouncing off the protection you've built for yourself.

You have the choice to collect or dismiss the things people say about you. At the same time, you get to decide what you say about yourself. The inner dialogue and the things you say to others about yourself will define the amount of power you get to carry every day.

> *Your inner dialogue should be guarded closely because as heavy as the weight of others' words can be, you are with your own thoughts 24 hours a day, with no breaks. If you're allowing the negative dialogue and name-calling to go on unsupervised in your head, you're just as responsible for forfeiting your power.*

You get to reframe the painful things you've thought and those hurtful things they've said in a way that actually strengthens you. And you get to decide that their opinions are irrelevant because ultimately, they are given that you are always the one in control.

So while the compliments feel good and likely resonate because they're probably *true* about you, it's still you who decides to appreciate and own all the things that make you so powerful. It's all up to you.

Remember how I mentioned in the introduction that I've created some bonuses throughout the book for you? Well here we go! I mean, I'm pumped you're reading this and I hope that it's sparking something inside you already, but we can do better, can't we?

How 'bout we put this information to work so it doesn't become one of those cool things you read one time. You deserve better than that. Let's start identifying how you feel about your power so you can take actual steps, today, to improve it, no matter which level of ownership you have in your power.

Scan this QR code to get access to your bonus tools that accompany this book.

Scan Me!

There's a reason I want you to pause to complete the bonus tools whenever they're mentioned. It's because I *really do* want you to experience the exponential increase that happens when you show up for yourself fully and expect powerful change.

After you click that link, activate the bonus tools for 10 minutes or so, it'll be a great time to hop back in and dive into chapter 2, cuz it's a doozy!

CHAPTER 2

IT'S NOT A SCAR, IT'S GOLD

It's said that Ashikaga Yoshimasa, a shogun in Japan around the late fifteenth century, had broken his favorite teacup and wanted it repaired. The story goes that his cup was sent to China for repair, which was typical at the time, but it was returned looking rough, with metal staples to join the cracks.

The shogun's craftsmen decided that instead of using the typical resin to glue the pottery back together, they'd honor him by mixing gold dust into the resin so that the cracks would become more beautiful once the pieces were joined together again. The shogun loved it and this new approach to fine pottery repair became a cultural art form.

This Japanese art form is known as *Kintsugi*. Masters continue to restore pottery in this way even today, creating more unique and even more valuable pieces that are often sold as high-ticket works of art. This beautiful Japanese practice doesn't just reassemble the broken pottery, it highlights and accentuates the broken parts, drawing attention to, and illuminating, the beauty of each scar. The philosophy behind Kintsugi is that nothing is ever truly broken.

The metaphor translates so obviously and effortlessly into the human experience. That despite feeling broken, we have the ability to repair, and when we choose to repair, a scar is formed. We can then allow our scars to become a beautiful, and unique attribute, making us even more valuable than before. It implies that our scars shouldn't be hidden and we shouldn't be ashamed of them. Instead, they should be on display for others to benefit from. This is the beauty of resilience.

Our accidents and accomplishments bring both emotional and physical scars. Those scars define us even more uniquely. They all tell a story.

Too often, though, our scars stay hidden out of fear of judgment from others. But if we chose to highlight our scars, put them on display like the beautiful Japanese pottery, and let it be okay for people to see them and learn about them, something amazing would happen. It could be like a human art exhibit, serving an even greater purpose than just beauty; it would inject inspiration and power to those who saw

Some people do operate this way, and it's incredible to witness. They enjoy the benefits of feeling free from the shame of hiding their scars, along with the knowledge that others are benefitting from the story we've told. They claim their role as the hero in their own story.

YOU are the main character...

Whether you like it or not, you're also the hero of your own life story, the main character. Many people find it hard to identify as the main character of anything. We've grown up on stories and films featuring larger-than-life characters, champions that we've admired, and even grown-ups wishing we could be like. No wonder it feels too big a title to be worthy of.

But when you think about how the main character starts out in any story, they're usually pretty regular. They're not especially captivating, although they might have some uniqueness or quiet charm that's appealing to the reader. The great transformation for these eventual heroes is in the gritty life disruptions, emergencies, traumas, or danger they battle through within the storyline.

These uninvited experiences forced them to level up in order to come out victorious on the other side. Their character traits became tested in hopes of bringing out the best of who they were; their courage, heart, endurance, perseverance, and inner strength, all being challenged. And while they're still the same person by the end of the story, they're a fortified version of themselves. They're enhanced and armed with new strengths to get them through the next big thing.

The same is true for you. With each new uninvited challenge life delivers, you're more equipped and better able to face it with confidence, knowing that you've been through some things that make you qualified for what you're about to face.

You *are* the hero of your life's story. And I know you've been through some hard things. Impossible things, even. I know that if you were to take inventory of every conflict, from the small to the impossible, and look at what you were forced to become through it, you might see that you're a lot more powerful than you give yourself credit for.

The most extreme challenges are sometimes the most painful. The times where so much grief and loss remains in us that we almost don't know where to put all the sadness. When we think about those challenges from our life stories, most of what we feel is the pain we encountered due to the immense size of the loss.

We don't usually allow ourselves to look at how much strength we gained just to get through it, because if we allowed ourselves to gain anything at all from that loss, it would be like saying we were glad for the loss to happen in order to become stronger.

Of course, that's not true and of course, we didn't want the loss to happen.

But what I've found through my own stories of loss and pain, after enough grieving and mourning has taken place, I can see how it changed me. If it was a person I'd lost, in the end, I've decided to pay tribute to them by allowing myself the strength I've gained through it all, because it takes more power to go on living while carrying their loss.

And to know that I didn't ask for this loss but I refuse to let it be for nothing. That instead, I'd honor them by becoming something greater than before, because if I allow myself to grow in times like these, I'm more valuable to the people around me.

We're so connected through suffering in these ways. Whether it's the loss of someone we love, the treatment we've received from someone else, a physical or mental ailment that makes life more difficult. Whether it's financial suffering or a spiritual drought, we all share in the feeling of what it's like to hurt this way.

There's also another kind of suffering. The suffering we create. This particular brand of suffering is the hardest to swallow since the pain of what's happening is bad enough, but knowing we were responsible for it is almost too much for our ego to bear.

This is where blaming others comes easiest. Another thing we tend to do is spin the story to make us look a little less terrible than the truth might expose, usually because we're still in victim and protection mode. And we can live in that false reality for a while but the shame and guilt never really disappear; in most cases, it gets worse.

So when we're brave enough to own our part in a story that went wrong, and share it with others, despite the fact that this truer version of events is highly unflattering, something happens.

The burden of shame starts to lift. You've let it out and shared it with people whom you trusted not to hurt you with it. You've allowed them to see that they're not alone in whatever pain they're going through while giving them permission to be real and honest with their own stories. Without sharing these things, we feel so alone. Our brain loves to tell us that *"There couldn't possibly be anyone else going through something like this."* This is the type of lie you believe which ends up isolating you even more.

Instead, you've powerfully become the example of what bravery looks like in an everyday situation. Bravery isn't just for the battlefield or the first responders (although they're out there doing it big on the daily *and* have the everyday bravery to show up for too). It's for all of us.

There is so much power found in the unflattering parts of our story when we use those stories to encourage others. When we're willing to share truths about ourselves that we aren't proud of, we're automatically the brave ones in the room because it's more natural to try and protect ourselves from harmful things, like our own story being used against us.

Just imagine a world where, once someone has healed from their trauma, their suffering, their pain, that they would feel no shame in sharing and teaching others about the experience. Imagine that this was such a common practice that it became effortless for people to share, habitually and culturally. Imagine that everyone is sharing these warning lessons and triumphs in numbers so big, that it would seem inevitable to everyone that scars will happen.

But that it wouldn't be something to fear because, just look at all these people surviving things, being okay with it, sharing what they've learned from it, and helping others through it.

If you could imagine a culture like that, can you also imagine how much courage we would have to take a chance on things we would normally fear? When you have an entire community of people who openly share about these things, and yet still come together to enjoy life and encourage others, there would be so much less to fear and so much more opportunity to see.

This is what makes your own hero's journey so powerful. You have a nucleus of people around you located within an entire community of others who share your environment, surrounded by a worldwide network of people you share connections with. This life of yours can inspire so many more, through the good and the bad you've pulled through.

This isn't about putting your private life on blast to social media. This is about, humility aside, recognizing that your story is powerful enough to inspire people on your own terms. And that you have access to people all around the globe, should you decide to share those experiences as a warning, a lesson, or an inspiration, even to just one.

You don't even need to head over to the internet to find women who've inspired you. I know you know people in your family, your church, your neighborhood, your school, work, or the grocery store, who've shown you how beautiful it can look to make it through something without identifying as a victim.

People who are literal definitions of the word "victim" yet would never, ever use that term on themselves. People who've been through something way tougher in life than you have and still show up every day trying to find a way to help others. People who've experienced financial hardship so extreme yet still prioritize generosity to others in a way that makes you feel joyfully compelled to give more.

These are the women who inspire us deeply. The women from our own lives allow us to witness how real their story is, maybe daily, or multiple times a week. Those women and their power to get through things, rise above it all, let go of the past, positively reframe the narrative on what they've been faced with. Simply hearing the names of these women referenced in our social circle is enough to remind us of how strong we can be. When the heroes are close to us, the impact of their power becomes more real. It seems more attainable and more manageable because we can witness it and they've shown us how to do it.

This is all the evidence you need to support the power of your own hero's journey. Your experiences and perspective are worthy. Your life is worthy. You are worthy, just because you are. Your positive experiences don't enhance your worthiness, just like the negative experiences (even the ones you feel responsible for) don't make you any less worthy either.

So even if you never shared it with the world, just knowing that there is so much power in your story, is enough to make you start showing up like the version of yourself you've earned along this way. Your experiences have shaped who you are today, for the good and the bad. Instead of running from those or hiding them under a blanket of shame, use them to your advantage by deciding to see what you've come through. And when you can, bring those stories to light, you're allowing your scars to become the golden resin that glued you back together for others to admire and benefit from.

Your old beliefs may have had power over you but you get to decide to take that power back, you beautiful Japanese pottery, you. *That's* the woman your family deserves. *That's* the woman your community deserves, and *that's* the woman this world so desperately needs.

Do you wanna see the ways you've made an impact that matters to this world? Well even if you think your negative experiences are dark enough to outweigh the good you've tried to create in the world, I've got good news. There's a tool to illuminate this for you with some metrics you can attach and it's about to unlock some amazing truth about your life.

How 'bout finding out which ways your scars made you more powerful? Well whadya know?

You've got some bonus content for both of these topics covered in chapter two, and you can grab them at using the QR code I've littered throughout this book

(and here's another one!)

Scan Me!

Again, you'll want to dive in and do this, not for me, but because *you* are about to start getting fueled through rediscovering the core of what makes you so incredibly powerful.

CHAPTER 3

FROM PAIN TO POWER

In less than 24 hours I received 255 comments and 125 reactions to my post.

Before publishing this book, I posted 4 options for book covers I'd narrowed down from a selection of over 310.

I was super excited to find out which design was resonating with the amazing women in my network and couldn't wait to meet them in the comments.

But what I wasn't expecting was to get a "heart" on the post from a woman who's never interacted with any of my content, ever.

Not once.

She *did,* however, welcome me to my new middle school years ago by making sure I didn't forget who she was.

If you've never had to adjust to a new school growing up, it's one of the most nerve-wracking experiences you can go through. If you had it like me, you woke up feeling insecure about the way you looked and wondered whether this new city and state appreciated the fashion sense that was accepted by your old friends back home.

You definitely didn't try to draw attention to yourself and potentially trigger an alpha cool kid who felt challenged by your confidence. No. You sit your awkward self down in the corner of that diesel-diffusing public transportation and hope you enjoy an entirely uneventful ride.

But my awkward outfits, buck teeth, flat chest, and ultra-thin hair must have been like catnip because most days, a girl, two years older than me, who sat with the cool crowd in the back of the bus, found a way to entertain her fans by loudly shaming me with her razor-sharp Neanderthal wit.

I had started to make a few friends in this new school, but none of them were on my bus to defend me when she started her commentary. And honestly, that year of my life was not the glow-up I was hoping for. It was more like the dull-down that most middle schoolers experience at some point; the year where you "accidentally lose" your school photos instead of bringing them home to your parents because there is no way you're letting those bad boys circulate into the family albums. So couple that with being the new kid and you're more or less a social leper.

This bully on the bus wasn't clever and didn't even seem like she was popular, actually, but she wasn't afraid to be the loudest. She made it crystal clear that she had *decided* she'd be the one in charge, even if it meant influencing a group of insecure, prepubescent misfits.

Every day I made myself as small as I could, squeezing into the corner of my seat, trying my hardest to avoid another targeted attack by this walking mean streak of a teenager. Listen, I know I was awkward looking compared to the cute girls in school. Besides, I'd been new to a school so many times before so I was familiar with the ol' *"lay low and be cool until you naturally find your people"* method. I tried to be relatively invisible. It was my trusted strategy for new-school-acclimation, and it had always worked before.

But at least once a week, she'd call me out, not by name of course, but by a fun title she decided I'd get that day; "Chester", or "horse mouth", or "pig face". I never really did know if she was talking to me because she called people all kinds of names, so when I didn't react or respond to her heckling, she'd go louder or come closer and make sure to punish me for not responding with a crueler comment than normal.

Her cronies would laugh way louder than her comment warranted, and I would turn back around, jaw clenched, staring out the window trying not to cry until the bus finally pulled up to my house.

She wasn't the first person to make me feel helpless, weak, unlovable, or alone, but she *was* the most vocal and she made the heaviest impression, as she rallied the others to join in while she chose a target from my menu of flaws.

This was how she chose to wield her power.

By the time I got to the ninth grade, I was playing Varsity sports, which meant I was accepted by my popular and beautiful student-athlete teammates. My braces were gone. I was honor-roll every quarter, and I'm pretty sure I sprouted a few more wisps of hair on my head (but just barely). So things were looking up.

I finally had some street cred. And because the humiliation of the bullying I received took such a toll on me, I decided that instead of wasting my newfound popularity, I'd show people you can be popular *and* kind. As an athlete accepted by teammates more popular than me, I finally felt powerful enough to stick up for others since my cooler friends would have my back.

I'd found some courage to do the right thing and help the kids who were more obvious targets for the predators in the hallway. I could help the victims by letting them know that someone cared. Even if we weren't really friends, they'd *get* that they were worth standing up to a bully for.

And that's when I realized I had more power than I knew. Except power didn't have to look like cruelty. It could look like protection, love, and bravery.

Now decades later, my adult brain can scan my former enemy's social media page and deduce a few uncomfortable truths about her life. Things I now realize must have made her feel the need to attack others first before they found out who she really was and expose her weaknesses to the crowd. She made sure people feared her, and it was an effective defense mechanism for her.

Those memories of humiliation have come back to visit over the years and I often hoped that eventually, it wouldn't hurt anymore to remember.

But sometimes it does because when I think about those times in detail, I can see the young, scared Sandra and I can feel what she felt all over again. The difference is that now I know if it weren't for the suffering I experienced, I might have never been brave enough to stand up for the kids who needed someone to be strong for them.

Years later, my roommate and I were hanging out one weekend in college, killing time by entertaining ourselves with baby name lists we found online. You know the ones, "this year's most popular", "most unique", "hardest to pronounce", and "most interesting celebrity baby names".

We picked our top 3 and at some point, we decided to look up the meaning of our own names on Wikipedia(listed below). This was an awareness moment for me that felt so powerful. It gave me a new sense of importance and caused me to reflect back on how the meaning of my name might really be true for me.

Sandra is a female name, which is often used as a short form for Alexandra or Cassandra.[1] Alexandra is a feminine form of the male name Alexander, generally interpreted to mean "protector of man" or "defender of man".

This made me smile and I decided to receive this new information as one extra wink from God letting me know I was strong enough for the experiences I'd been through and it made me feel a little protected, in a way.

When you take the time to sit with the pain from your past, you can look at it for what it really is. Most often it's the result of someone else's decisions or behavior, which was born out of the pain *they* received. And it's easy to see how this cycle has the ability to become a generational curse if we let it.

This doesn't mean the pain someone inflicted on you was ever okay or even justified, but you get to decide that this pain from your past doesn't define who you are. It doesn't get to rob you of an ounce of your power. It doesn't make you less worthy, and it certainly doesn't make you unlovable. All it did was knock your perspective off course about who you really are.

The good news is that there's a way to get back on course and reclaim your power. A way where you aren't burdened by the false stories that you've adopted as your truth along the journey.

I accidentally created a practice that has empowered me to substantially shift my outlook around who I am. It's simple and brief, but compounded over time with consistency has been an absolute game-changer for me. Here's how it works;

Tuning out with headphones and white noise, getting in my car, locking myself in the bathroom, whatever it takes to focus, little by little, day by day, for as long as I can (with the goal being no more than about 10 minutes).

Concentrating on the traits, experiences, friendships, victories, accomplishments, compliments, surprises, sacred moments, and joy that fills in the rest of my memories throughout my life. Allowing these memories and truths to seep back into my awareness.

When I do, sometimes memories that have been buried for years come up, filling in the gaps and bringing even more truth to the surface about who I am. My brain is performing confirmation bias by finding the evidence to support the intention, something our brains are expert at doing.

This is why it gets easier and easier to feel your way towards a better opinion about what that your pain or suffering gets to mean about you. You get to decide to look back at it from the perspective of having come out the other side while remembering all the incredible traits that make you who you are.

Peer or family criticism starts in childhood and yet the majority of small humans aren't raised with emotional healing training and healthy coping mechanisms, so it's usually work we have to start doing when we become aware of the experiences that have shaped us in a way that no longer serves us.

This is something I've become conscious of as my kids have begun to grow. The importance of reaching down and walking their negative experiences out with them in a way that allows them to manage and filter things that don't feel good to them. It's one way to help shift the emotional health for the next generation.

So if you feel that this particular exercise has helped you, it might be helpful to the younger humans in your life to understand how they might turn their own pain into power, allowing you to become the trusted guide they need to help them through it.

CHAPTER 4

FEEDBACK IN THE FAILURE

My name was called to head down to the conference room. I started walking that way, excited because it's been a little over a week since I helped close a multi-million dollar deal in commercial real estate. It was bonus time.

Our company always did the best cakes for everyone's birthdays so I was pretty sure I could count on that, after all, this was the biggest deal anyone had closed in a long time. So definitely cake, but maybe balloons and champagne. Yeah, that would definitely warrant the occasion.

As I'm walking down the hall, I noticed that all the desks and offices were empty. This could only mean one thing; they were *all* waiting for me in the conference room. At this point, I'm thinking we'll all probably end up having cake and a glass of champagne and going home early because, hey, it was Friday after all.

But when I opened the door to the conference room, there was only one person there. It was one of the owners sitting down across the table from me. No balloons, no champagne, and no cake. His expression was flat and my stomach sank.

What in the eff was going on?

Instead of the bonus I'd been expecting, I was asked to sit down so he could explain the terms of my severance. They were letting me go. The only salesperson in the company. I was the workhorse, working late, bringing my jobs home with me, completing projects over the weekend, taking on responsibilities beyond my title because the company needed help. Trying to wrap my head around why a real estate closing of that size, signed with a substantial global company, would ever warrant a termination.

I never got my answer. When I asked, I was given the standard, "the company is going in a different direction" answer, which was clearly confusing since my entire job was to sell things so they could make money. There I was, selling things, making them tons of money, so what kind of direction are they planning on taking this? To me, this seemed like the answer you'd give someone if you either didn't know the truth or you were afraid to say it. Either way, I was seething and left with unanswered questions.

I felt sick, but numb at the same time, as I packed my desk up in a banker's box (turns out the movies had that right...they really *do* give you a banker's box to shove your stuff in and do the walk of shame to the parking lot).

It later occurred to me that they'd let all the employees go early that day in order to minimize the damage in case I snapped when they fired me. So I was wrong about the reason for getting called into the boardroom, but I was right about one thing; they did let us all go home early that Friday.

For almost a decade, I couldn't say the words, "I got fired". I had to soften it when referencing my experience by saying things instead, like, "I was let go", or "they laid me off", or "they sent me home with a severance" because the thought of saying the words, "I got fired", sounded too harsh of a failure than I felt I ever could have deserved.

I'd worked way too hard in this misogynistic boys club of an industry and made my own way. I'd worked on weekends as a single mom and found a way to make sure my kids were taken care of, nurtured, and loved while getting all the extra projects and side jobs done that they asked for. Because it was never explicit, but always implied, that if it wasn't completed over the weekend, my value in the company would be in question.

So I always figured out a way to rise to the occasion and get produce high-quality work, no matter what. So the idea that I might be fired by any company at all was something I never thought I'd ever have to face.

Especially since the trusted route in life, the safe and secure approach to choosing a career, was to go to college, get the finance degree, secure the job in real estate, climb the ladder, bank the retirement, and just ride it out, with all the benefits until you reach retirement.

But as it turned out, that security blanket I'd expected, wasn't the fleece and wool cozy combo my peers and I had been led to believe for all those years growing up. It was more like a mosquito net and it tore apart after just a few seasons.

After hundreds of fruitless job applications and two young kids at home, my options were limited so I decided to entertain freelancing work in branding packages, marketing build-outs, and website design. I hated the idea of becoming a business owner but freelancing didn't feel like that. Those were *side jobs*. Those didn't count (right?).

During this time I got remarried and when my husband, who's a chiropractor, decided he was sick of working for other doctors and wanted to open up a wellness clinic of his own, he asked me if I could do that with him. Doctors are trained in their specialty, not in business, so they typically go into practice with some form of manager or business partner.

I knew absolutely nothing about opening a clinic of any kind but I also knew that side job freelancing in the way I was approaching it wasn't going to be sustainable for me. I'd always known I never wanted to own my own business but given the circumstances, the lack of employment despite my efforts, and the fact that I wasn't going into this alone, I had just enough courage to take this project on.

So with a $10,000 line of credit, a month-to-month lease, and 8-months pregnant with my third child, we started doing the construction on the office with the help of family and friends.

We made only the necessary modifications to this old 1,000 square foot building and purchased the equipment, supplies, software, and hardware needed to run the clinic.

Somehow, in just 8 weeks, we were able to open. And with no daycare options available, a staff of two (my husband and me), I strapped my 6-week old baby to my chest in a fabric wrap and went to work every day.

I greeted every single patient, checked them in, conducted consults, took phone calls, changed diapers, completed paperwork, accepted payments, dealt with bookings and reschedules, nursed my son, marketed the business online, threw some lunch down the hatch, and hunted for answers to questions I had about how I could turn this startup into a successful operation.

We had heard from nearly every industry professional in the area that it was a major risk to open a clinic that didn't take insurance, that Western New York wasn't the place for it. We were told that starting your own practice in an area with as many healthcare options would be an uphill battle we might not want to fight.

People warned us that the patients wouldn't understand or accept the concept of paying out of pocket for healthcare (even though our model rivaled their copays or better in many cases). We were told there was no way we could turn a profit within 3 years, but more likely not within 5.

This felt a lot like what people mean when they say "trial by fire". Because by the time my son was 14 months old, I was delivering my fourth child. I secured a spot at a daycare nearby for my 14-month-old and strapped baby number four in the fabric wrap while hitting 6 figures just after 12 months in business. Even though they said it couldn't be done.

We did it all again for one more year and when my youngest turned one year old, he joined his brother in daycare and we moved into a new location, having doubled our patient base from the previous year.

The thing is, I never wanted to be a business owner. I never would have done it. But it took getting fired, what I had believed to be, my biggest failure, in order to initiate this huge life change. Creating my own business allowed me to do some things I never thought would be possible.

I was able to bring my youngest kids to work and spend the entire first year of life with both of them, which was a privilege I didn't have with my oldest two children.

I was able to help create an entire full-service clinic, with standardized operating procedures, customized care packages, a new approach to patient care in our area, featuring services no one else could offer yet.

I was able to take every skill I'd learned, up to that point, along with every mistake I knew to avoid and build a successful business from scratch. A business that no one else thought would work, in an area where it really shouldn't have, and turn a profit just after one year, with no investors, no real capital, and a baby strapped to me for 24 months straight.

But the most important thing that happened during this time was transforming my anger and resentment from having been fired into gratitude and appreciation, thanking God that I was fired, literally. When I allowed myself to admit it, I knew that I never would have left unless they made me. That was when I finally understood that my biggest failure, turned out to be one of my biggest blessings.

Today, I can talk about getting fired, and I do. Often. Because it doesn't hurt anymore now that I can see how necessary it was in my journey. That hindsight is really something, isn't it? I don't feel shame anymore when I think about losing my job because I know now that it had nothing to do with my value and worth as a person.

I also know that it allowed me to become a better and more successful woman, who is now able to reach so many more people with a message that can actually make a difference in their lives. I wasn't ever able to do that in my old career.

I found a new version of myself in the failure of getting fired. I was forced to burn down the smaller, more insecure design (the one that was willing to settle for good enough), and allow her to take the phoenix approach and become reborn as a more powerful version she hadn't yet met.

Think about the word "failure" and how much weight it carries; It even sounds heavy, like an onomatopoeia.

So imagine you're taking inventory of all of these stories in your past and labeling them as failures.

How heavy is that to carry around? How does the weight of those affect decisions related to those perceived failures you had in the past?

For instance, I've worked with thousands of women who own their own business and say one of those women perceived all of her past business attempts as failures. What do you think happens in her body and in her decision-making when someone comes to her with a great business opportunity?

She doesn't look at that opportunity with hope, excitement, or faith in her future success. She looks at it with fear and discouragement.

The weight of the word failure is holding you back. Not just from the business but from relationships, from getting healthier, from life in general.

You didn't fail. You just lived and experienced. The journey was never supposed to be perfect. And oh by the way, who the eff are you gonna inspire with a flawless, blemish-free history? Who are you going to relate to? Who are you going to comfort? What advice can you offer others if you've never gone through anything challenging? And how boring would that be?

No one's writing a book about that life and no one's making a film about that life. So if we can get on board with the idea that it wasn't even a failure, but instead, a valuable chapter in your life, equipping you and for greater things, doesn't that feel better? Doesn't that feel more hopeful? And isn't that just more true?

If the information above were the equivalent of cleaning out a wound, then the information to follow might equate to a salve to support healing growth over the wound.

Going one step further, with the aim to empower you from old experiences, when you look at your past, pinpointing any of your perceived failures, ask yourself what those challenges allowed you to become.

What did they allow you to learn?

Who did they allow you to meet?

How did they change your perspective for the better?

Which benefits would you be missing if those things had never happened?

You might also be looking at the past through a distorted lens. What if you were looking at it in a more dramatic light, which subconsciously allowed you to adopt more of a victim role for a moment so that your ego wouldn't feel so bruised?

What if it wasn't even so much of a failure as it was an interruption?

What if it wasn't a failure, but a setback?

Was it really a failure or was it a misunderstanding?

Was it a failure or was it a traumatic event that you're healing from?

What's a better word than "failure" for what happened in your past?

All of the answers that you come up with are feedback for you. This is why I don't subscribe to the same definition of "failure" as I used to. I believe now, that there are only two ways I can actually fail.

1. If I never try
2. If I give up on something I truly want (*disclaimer: this particular mention does*

*not cover divorce, in my opinion. I'm
referring here to only things which you're
passionate about or believe and hope for
in a way that will improve your life)*

So if that's true then anything else is nothing more
than an incredible lesson, a new set of tools, an
encouraging story, or a warning for others. It gets
to be better than what you've been telling
yourself. It gets to be reframed. It doesn't mean
that something bad didn't happen, but you have
the ability to tell a new story around what
happened in your past.

You can do this without lying to yourself, but by
shedding some retrospective light on the event so
it doesn't have the type of power that might have
been keeping you small. Allowing yourself to view
the past with some helpful framing can lighten
the heaviness that that word "failure" carries.
That's what makes you the hero. You've been
through something tough, probably a ton of
things that were tough. But you got through it and
you kept going. You didn't let it stop you. You
might have even tried again on the thing you
thought you failed at. To finally create a success
out of it.

Hypothetical case study time!

Okay, over the course of my career I've worked with thousands of women who own their own business and let's imagine one of those women perceived all of her past business attempts as failures. She never learned to reframe the events in her life. She allowed the defeat to consume her. She doubted every move she made because of them and she always had some level of fear tagging along during the waking hours of her day.

What do you think happens in her body and in her decision-making when someone comes to her with a great business opportunity?

She's not gonna look at that with hope, excitement, and an expectation of success.

She looks at it with fear and discouragement, believing she'd only embarrass herself if she tried since she'd probably fail at that too. Even though the more likely scenario is that she'd be perfect for this opportunity and has all the skills and heart to knock it out of the park.

This particular mention might be hypothetical but it's a real-life obstacle holding women back every day, and I witness it.

Missed opportunities like that are so expensive. Not just from a business angle, but it costs your spirit something every time doubt and fear win. It's like a little bit of your power gets chiseled off your theoretical armor each time a decision is made from fear.

The weight of the word failure is holding you back. Not just from work-life and business opportunities but from every area of life, including relationships, getting healthier, finding joy.

So what if you decided to believe that you didn't fail, you just lived and experienced. That the journey was never supposed to be perfect. Never. And oh by the way, who the eff are you gonna inspire with a flawless, blemish-free history?

Who are you gonna relate to?

Who are you going to comfort?

What tools and advice can you help people with if you've never gone through anything and how BORING would that be anyway?

No one's writing a book about that life.

No one's making a film about that life.

So if you can get on board with that, it shouldn't be a stretch to take it one step further and see those experiences as valuable life chapters which equipped you and others for greater things.

Doesn't that feel better?

Doesn't that feel more hopeful?

So my former failures are now referred to by me as "perceived failures", since I can see how it all played out and it wasn't a failure at all. It was a critical event that allowed me to become something greater and do something bigger with my life. This was never a failure at all, my ego just never let me see it at the time.

When you decide to reframe your failures and look at them as feedback, you're able to learn from every situation. It might take time for emotions to settle after a perceived failure, but if you can at least appreciate that, while emotions are still high, soon enough you'll see this event as a catalyst for the next better thing.

You already know that diamonds would never be created without immense pressure over time. And that gold would be almost worthless without the excruciating heat of the fire that's required to refine it to purity. You know that great wine and the world's best olive oil can't exist without destroying the fruit that it came from, and you are no different.

You will continue to go through harsh things, you will feel pressure, you will feel tested, and you will get squeezed, but those experiences don't all need to be classified as failures. When they happen, you have a choice to see these difficulties as punishment and pain, or as the process of refinement required to transform you into an even more valuable and powerful asset to this world.

And when it is a failure of never trying or simply giving up, there's a lesson there too. A lesson that teaches you where your fear and doubt lies, or about what you truly don't believe in anymore. It has the ability to highlight where you might need to fortify or forgive yourself. Or show you that you might need to stop comparing in order to make an attempt at the goal you're hoping to go after.

So no matter what the experience was, no matter what you went through, there is power in it if you choose to see it that way.

They said it…

 TMD

⭐⭐⭐⭐⭐ Verified Purchase

LOVED this book!!

Reviewed in Canada on September 1, 2021

Heard Sandra first speak at a Tony Robbins event last fall and loved her energy, honesty, cut through the crap personality and approach to life. Why can't you build an amazing business and have fun and sanity at the same time??!!! Her approach to business, wisdom that has helped our business so much and wonderful personality shine through in her new book.

 Marah Elisabeth Förster

⭐⭐⭐⭐⭐ Verifizierter Kauf

Exceptional

Rezension aus Deutschland vom 1. September 2021

Sandra Haseley's Power Method is an easy to read heartfelt uplift to every single woman on this planet:
She reframes power and leadership into soft skills every woman embodies and leaves no one behind. I got a power boost reading her kind and uplifting words. The bonus material truly brings it into life. My deepest admiration for this amazing woman, standing heart to heart with all woman around the globe.
If we all took this lessons in deeply, this would mean a transformational shift for wo/menkind 🙏💙

 MATTKIRK2

⭐⭐⭐⭐⭐ Verified Purchase

Short, easy, POWERful read!

Reviewed in the United States on September 2, 2021

Sandra seamlessly weaves the art of story telling with practical strategies to ignite the most powerful version of you. I highly recommend this book to any woman who has ever felt she was meant for more. I love the way Sandra comes alongside you, making you feel like you can breakthrough any obstacle in your way…plus she gives you the practical tools to actually breakthrough the obstacles! Do yourself a favor and have this book in your arsenal of awesomeness!

PART II | LEGEND-LIKE LEADERSHIP

lead·er·ship

/ˈlēdərˌSHip/

noun

1. the action of leading a group of people or an organization.
    "different styles of leadership"
2. the state or position of being a leader.
    "the leadership of the party"

   -Oxford Languages

Follow the leader, or maybe DON'T?

I'm taking it on as my job for the next few chapters to show you how and why you need to develop the leadership skills that are buried inside you and unapologetically claim ownership of who you are. That said, I'll start with this;

You're a *gift* to this world, and your skills and capabilities were never for you to keep. They were given to you to be shared with the world, to bless the daylights out of people around you, and inspire others to share the gifts that *they* have, too.

You've been exposed to and learned from so many leaders in your life, from childhood all the way through adulthood ranging from your home, the classroom, your workplace, and your community. You may not have ever taken the time to identify which kind of leader you'd like to embody, especially if you haven't yet classified *yourself* as a leader.

That's about to change, so buckle up, buttercup.

What I want you to come away with from this next section is the awareness of how important it is to lead yourself, in order to be an effective leader to anyone else. It's the thing all leaders have in common, regardless of their style.

CHAPTER 5

SHE'S NOT A LEADER, SHE'S A GIRL!

I imagine that most of us have a similar idea when we hear the word, "leader". We imagine someone who's in charge, someone powerful, someone brave. These words have become somewhat synonymous with each other somewhere along the way. Oh, and if we're being honest, I'd bet most people would imagine this leader as a man.

That's because traditionally speaking, most of the names who've gone down in history in cultures across the world, have operated inside this framework of leadership and frequently share these qualities. These are the type of leaders who successfully lead their followers.

I never really questioned this imagery of leadership until recent years. I'd always had female heroes that I looked up to in my life, in sports, business, world politics, art, and science. But it wasn't until I became a full-time entrepreneur and built a community of strong, brilliant, beautiful, loving women across the world that my paradigm started to shift.

The more women I met, the more stories I heard, and the more moved I became. I met refugees who'd moved to America quite literally escaping with only their lives and zero money, each now running an incredible business and giving back in massive ways.

I met a woman who'd lost her home in a natural disaster, along with many of her family members, who later rebuilt and created a life from scratch with deep intention, purpose, and wealth. And my list of connections like these continues to grow longer every single week.

I've met women who've endured patterns of intense trauma and injury throughout their lives, who've fled from their dangerous environments. The same women who refuse to see themselves as victims, but instead share their stories to warn, encourage, and inspire other women.

Although these women aren't celebrities or massive influencers, in my eyes they're so powerful for having gone through what they did, becoming wiser, stronger, and more generous.

Through day-to-day business networking, I was introduced to new women each week who offered a new and unique testimony of their journey as we got to know each other. As I listened, I couldn't help but find leadership woven into their story, even though none of them had ever claimed the title of "leader" as they spoke. These women were humble, driven, and inspiring.

Around the same time they started orbiting my social media network, I started to wonder why these women were such evident leaders to me even though their qualities didn't align with the traditional paradigm of male leadership. I was amazed when I realized it was actually the *feminine* aspects they all embodied which allowed me to see them as leaders.

Not gonna lie, this one broke my brain for a bit and had me asking myself things like,

"Are these women actually inspirational leaders, or was I just moved by their stories, making them out to be leaders because they were so likable?"

And,

"Feminine qualities have never been universally associated with strong or effective leadership so I had to be wrong about this, didn't I?"

But I kept landing on the notion that it had to be true. The type of inspiration they cultivated in others wasn't just some warm-and-fuzzy anecdote followed by an, "*awwww, that's nice...*". If for no other reason than the fact that I absolutely identify as a leader and women like this were inspiring me to do more than simply feel something, they were inspiring me to *move.*

When you hear the raw, powerful, and gritty stories from women who were up against a wall in ways you've never been, in ways you doubt you might ever make it out alive, and here they are, never giving up, hand-crafting a new life for themselves and creating success. That's the kind of inspiration that ignites momentum in people, *especially* in other leaders.

Leadership started to register with me in a whole new way. If women were able to spark inspiration and momentum in *my* leadership activities without even knowing it, using a *feminine* approach, maybe I could modify my own leadership style into something that felt more natural to me.

I decided to take an analytical look at the women I was connected with who presented with strong leadership traits like the ones I mentioned above. If I was going to find a style to suit me best, I'd have to know which features I could start to shed and which ones I could lean into more to become a more effective leader, while maintaining a style that feels more comfortable to me.

I did my research online and cross-referenced what I found against the women I knew to see if the information aligned. It did and I couldn't have been more relieved and excited to discover that these feminine leadership descriptors were actually the same ones that society generally perceives as weaknesses.

The top feminine leadership qualities identified were:

Empathy

Vulnerability

Humility

Inclusiveness

Generosity

Balance

Patience

I mean, look at that list! These traditionally feminine qualities which have seemed soft for decades or more by society's standards are now showing up in the research data to be desired traits of company leaders. John Gerzema conducted a study with 64,000 people in 13 countries, with two-thirds of the participants stating they believed the world would be a better place if men thought more like women.

Now imagine a woman with all those traits who supports you and speaks into your life? This is a woman who speaks to leaders like you in a way that proves they value you. This is a leader who sees you, validates you, and allows you to be recognized for your zone of genius, unthreatened by your power and worth.

This woman is living out the meaning of the words on that list every day, and she's mentoring *you*. Leading you into your own greatness, not with force or coercion, but through being a living example of confidently standing in who she is, creating space for other women to develop their own brand of personal leadership. That's what it looks like to be a leader who leads other leaders.

When you choose to lead yourself, you're choosing to lead other leaders as well. The two can't be separated because it's through the witnessing of a woman powerfully leading herself, which encourages other women to model the same for their own lives.

What a relief it is to know that you don't have to put in effort for this approach to leadership, you simply have to show up as yourself, and others are made better as a result of your presence. You become the first domino that causes a chain reaction, knocking down the rest of the chain for as far as they can stretch.

In contrast, when we desire to be a leader out of ego, we behave in a way that makes sure we stay on a pillar above the others. This type of approach can nurture a toxic "God complex" in some traditional leaders, forcing an unhealthy working environment. It tends only to suit people who are more comfortable following, than leading.

The world needs followers and in no way should that title imply negative connotations, but followers in this type of environment often depend on these leaders, feeling as though they can't do much without them. This dynamic sets a "pedestal leader" up for potential burnout since they're now obligated to continually pour into everyone else without fail if they want anything to get done. If you're trying to lead in a way that doesn't include leaders among you, you'll be doing all of it yourself and you *will* hit a wall, eventually.

Lead the way, lady...

Leading yourself well means taking accountability for your work and life. Accountability is a willingness to own the results of your choices, actions, inactions, behaviors, thoughts, communication, and attitude. An accountable person doesn't waste time blaming others or making excuses.

When you hear the word "leadership", it's typically implying leadership over others, just like the definition, from Oxford Languages, spells out at the top of this section. But the definition just above this paragraph, taken from the State of Kentucky's personnel resource site, "the state or position of being a leader", is often overlooked. This part applies to what I mean when I say you need to lead *yourself*, which is what this chapter is going to explore.

You don't have to run an organization, be the head of a department, run a division or march in the streets to be a leader. Simply being a woman in this world is enough of a title to call on you to become the leader you were meant to be. A woman who interacts and makes moves like a leader among her colleagues, friends, community, the people in her home, the strangers in the store, and her network online.

None of these environments is any less or more important than the other in terms of your impact as a leader. You can inspire growth in people no matter where you find yourself, as long as you show up as *you*.

You may not consider yourself a leader, maybe in any category. And maybe that's due to your humble nature or worse, a self-deprecating habit in how you view yourself. If that's you, I'm gonna have to ask you to take out that trash and stop acting like you aren't a miracle walking. Because this has nothing to do with ego and everything to do with self-respect and responsibility. You may not see it like this, but I can't imagine a world where it's *not* your responsibility to be a leader among your people, wherever they happen to exist with you. You have gifts, intelligence, experience, heart, energy, and time to give so if you're not offering those to others, you're burying diamonds.

Great leaders are able to lead themselves into a better version of themselves and when people witness it, they're activated to find out a way they can do the same thing for themselves. So the mere act of you showing up in a way that's all-the-way-you, automatically makes you a leader in your environment. Stick with that.

When I first became a mother, I jumped back into the archives of all the advice I'd ever gotten from my mom. I could hear her voice in my ear to,

"sleep when the baby sleeps"

"lower your voice when they're raising theirs so they quiet down to hear you"

"clean as you go with them throughout the day so you can lie down at night and just relax", among thousands of other gems of wisdom.

I was willing to listen to my mother growing up because she was so great at being a mom and her advice never failed. So following her lead felt like a no-brainer. I was relieved to have her advice ready for when I had kids of my own. I mean, I'm literally the grown test product of what she raised and I'm not mad at it. Plus, I've spent decades reaping the benefits from applying her counsel throughout my life.

I didn't realize it until I had kids, but my mom spent my entire school-aged years training me up as a leader. She was hand-selecting advice for me, knowing what would best suit my personality and style while giving me context as to why I might want to take action on one thing or avoid something else.

She didn't speak in parables or anything but she framed the teachings she gave me throughout life around stories, metaphors, analogies, and background explanations so her kids wouldn't be the type of people to automatically agree just because "someone said so". She was raising analytical thinkers, the type of people who'd be equipped to lead others since she'd been grooming them to lead themselves.

I remember my mom telling me at one point when I was young that although she wanted us to be happy kids and have fun, as a mother, that wasn't her primary responsibility. She said, "I'm raising grown-ups. It's my job to make sure I do whatever I can to help you grow into amazing adults." So if she was ranking them, having fun came second to making sure she was raising the kind of adults she could be proud of.

That lesson was sobering to me because it was the first time I can remember being aware that my time as a kid wasn't going to last very long. Not if my mom's main job was to get me "adult-ready" by the time high school was over.   But it gave me a healthier perspective on rules in our house and why mom took our character building so seriously.

It's all fun and games...

When I was training in hopes of playing softball for Division 1 college, I needed to continue fine-tuning my fastpitch skills as a softball player. My parents didn't find me a coach who couldn't execute at an expert level. They put me in touch with a pitching specialist who was a nationally ranked men's fastpitch softball pitcher. He loved the game but he loved pitching even more.

As a pitcher on the mound, you're meant to lead the team on the defense. You can't lead others unless you can get up there, on your own, and lead yourself. The way I learned to do that was by taking instruction directly from a man who'd already led a team of grown men in that same way, at an expert level.

The pressure of being the center of attention on the mound during a game can be overwhelming and nerve-wracking on days where things just weren't going my way. Half the time I showed up for games I'd had some form of stress that was playing over in my mind, causing me to lose focus and doubt myself.

The less confident I became, the more mistakes I made. The more mistakes I made, the more tempting it became to wave the bench and get a relief pitcher to take my place. But sometimes I was able to lead myself to a better feeling by adjusting my mental game with some healthy perspective.

I'd start to think about the amount of time and dedication I'd invested into mastering my pitching skills. I thought about the people who invested their time in training me, including my parents who'd spent time, money, and energy to get me to and from these trainings over the years. I considered my teammates, who deserved better than a pitcher who's acting like Eeyore, and once in a while, I'd even remember that I was worth showing up for too.

When I was able to do this, I was able to incrementally improve my game, one pitch at a time, building back my confidence which often translated into a great performance throughout the rest of the game. And when my team started to see me catch my stride again on the mound, they felt the hope come back, and they'd start encouraging each other more. They played harder, they cheered louder, and they focused on the win.

This is just a small example of what it looks like to lead yourself in a way that encourages others to lead themselves. This measurable and tangible outcome wasn't created by a physical catalyst, it was born out of an invisible, private thought that snowballed into a shift in physical behavior, which inspired my teammates, and resulted in a win (...*most days*).

Your actions are a direct result of the thoughts you're thinking which is why leading yourself always starts in your mind. It goes like this;

The thoughts you think create feelings in your body and the feelings in your body trigger you to take a certain action, which leads you to a specific result.

This leadership approach of "leading leaders to lead" works in every area of your life, whether it's sports, church, work, relationships with your significant other, your children, or your friends.

When you choose to lead yourself through truly authentic behavior, being fully human, giving others permission to do the same, while they watch and model your example.

Acting fully human can happen when you're completely aware of your strengths without being conceited while being mindful of your weaknesses without assigning any shame to yourself. Instead of shirking compliments, you say "thank you", with grace instead. Rather than performing self-deprecation when one of your weaknesses is exposed, you let it go, knowing we're allowed to be powerful and imperfect at the same time.

Taking ownership of who you are, what you want, and how you want to show up, creates a spark that lights fires in others to do the same. It's like an unspoken permission that says, 'I'd act the same whether you were witnessing or not because this is exactly who I am; I do whatever I want, and you can too." Although no one ever needs permission to be themselves, a lot of us tend to hold back out of fear of judgment from others. This unspoken permission creates an environment where people can start to improve together because when you're around people who are so comfortable being fully themselves, it feels safe for you to do the same.

If you're the one showing up this way in your circle of people, just imagine how incredible it'll feel to watch your friends, coworkers, spouse, and kids start acting more like *themselves*. There's so much joy, connectedness, trust, and creativity when we feel safe to be whatever we are. All it takes is a leader who's not looking for followers, but one who's willing to be the first domino to fall.

CHAPTER 6

YOU'RE KINDA DIFFERENT, HUH?

The doctor picked up the swaddled and calm one-day-old infant, brought the baby over to a counter, where he pricked the heel of the baby's foot with a tiny needle for a standard blood screening. As soon as the needle touched the baby's heel, she shrieked at the top of her lungs in alarm, while the mother watched on, stifling her laughter.

The mother knew how small the pinprick was and the baby's reaction seemed incredibly dramatic for such a small poke. She'd said she knew right then, that this baby had a fire in her and that she could expect a lot more of that because this was clearly not a learned response, but part of her personality.

That mother was my mother, and that baby was me.

We've got nature and we've got nurture. We're all born with a unique personality and a set of strengths that come baked in, making some of us scream for a tiny needle poke, for instance. That's the nature piece. And along with our strengths, our weaker traits often get helped along or encouraged by the people around us or by the environment that we grow up in. That's the nurture side.

One of the personality traits that God decided to give me was the fire I've had all along. *Passion or enthusiasm* are probably better titles for the trait. I was never a dramatic child and I avoided confrontation wherever possible, both of which still apply to me today.

That hopeful and loving passion I had would show up in things I believed in and got excited about, but my passion also includes a fierce level of determination which would show up when things seemed unfair to me. Unfair for me or for others around me that I cared about.

I was enthusiastic while I was having fun with my friends or retelling a story that was interesting or comical to me, and I was always passionate about doing well in sports and being part of a team.

Sports was where I first found my place in leadership. My enthusiasm for my team's ability to do well compelled me to cheer loudly and encourage my teammates while they played. I happened to excel at sports so the combination of my encouraging behavior and skills in the game, often earned me the position of captain or co-captain.

I definitely wanted to win, but for me, more of the passion for the game came from knowing that my teammates deserved a win because I could see what they were capable of. I know how hard they worked and I wanted them to be as proud of themselves as I was of them. I always felt like they had my back and the teams I was a part of always felt like family. So when they weren't playing like I knew they could, encouragement seemed important in those moments. I believed that if they weren't playing at the level of their skill, they were obviously stuck mentally somehow, and I wanted to do what I could to help them get back to excellence.

I didn't realize it then, but I definitely know it now; that there are so many times where I might need to witness someone else believing in me in order for me to believe in myself. That if I have someone I trust and admire, who believes in me, I can borrow that belief until I get back to believing in myself. Like I owe them that for believing in me, and at the very least, that I could *try* for them.

Sports wasn't the only place I found this personality trait to be useful. I was working in high school at a movie theatre with a bunch of other teenagers, and we all got along pretty well. There were some quieter girls on the staff, meek but friendly. I was cleaning up around the corner from the breakroom and heard two of them talking on their break.

They were complaining about one of the managers and how uncomfortable they were around him. How he seemed like he was putting his hands on them to "gently move them out of the way" but he'd have his hands on their hips, or really low on their back. I didn't interrupt them because it was definitely a private conversation and I felt bad for overhearing, and since I hadn't noticed this before, I didn't feel I had anything to contribute. Instead, I decided to start paying attention over the next week while I was at work.

Now that I was looking, I could see it several times per shift. The unnecessary touching, the look on the girls' faces, and then it happened to me, just once, but enough to make me feel like I needed to take 17 showers in a row just to get the "gross" off.

I spoke to the girls I'd heard discussing it the week before and let them know I'd overheard what they'd complained about and that I, too, had complaints. I asked them to each write a letter describing their issue with the manager and that I'd talk to the other girls and see if they'd be willing to do the same. The letters were gathered and sent to corporate headquarters and about a week after that, we never saw the manager again.

This was during a time where it was uncommon to complain about things like this, and it felt like it'd be a stretch then, to believe that corporate would even do anything about it. Someone asked me later in my life why I hadn't gone to the police instead of "just talking to corporate". But the thought had only briefly crossed my mind back then, feeling as though the police would never deem our situation worthy of attention, so it felt like going to upper-level management was the only leverage we had.

The police may have taken us seriously at that time, in retrospect, but given what we knew and how the culture seemed to operate among young female harassment cases against older, respected white men in the workplace, we didn't believe we'd be heard. Although I now wish we would have gone to the police, I'm still glad we were able to feel safe at work again, and I'm proud of myself for having just enough courage to try and help where I could. It also planted a seed that even small displays of leadership could be so valuable in ways that were more important than just winning a game.

When you consider the times in your life where you had to make a choice to speak up, to act, to *not* act, to defend, to keep going, or to be an example, those are all times you've led yourself. Those were the times you didn't need someone to take over and lead you to a solution. The times where you listened to your gut and stood for something in that moment. Those are examples of leading yourself.

Rooting for your teammates when you can see them start to doubt themselves.

Banding together to make a plan to defend your right to feel safe in the workplace.

Standing up for someone who's an easy target and defending them against a bully for others to see.

These are some of the small examples in my life where I'd led myself. You have them too. You might have a different personality than I do, and I'm sure you have different strengths and weaknesses, but you also have unique life experiences that I never had. These experiences are archived in your memory somewhere and they helped to craft you into who you are today. And if you choose to, you can start pulling from your cranium's card catalog and bring up memories where you stepped into a powerful role by leading yourself.

These are experiences that tend to build us up with more courage, confidence, and energy for quite a while. But for most people, if you have a series of more defeating scenarios that play out after that, it can take the wind out of your sails from those moments when you *were* able to lead yourself. The more you remember the times of defeat, the quieter those times of triumph influence your self-identity.

If you could remember every single experience somehow and were to make a list of all the times you felt proud of how you showed up as a girl, lady, or woman, you'd likely be looking at something that resembles an ancient scroll. Say you were to attach a scoring system to this list based on the amount of positive impact you made on humans as a result of you showing up powerfully.

For each experience you listed, you assign a rating from 1-10, with 1 being the least amount of positive impact you made on humans and 10 being the maximum amount of positive impact possible. You add up the ratings from each one of those experiences and get a total weighted score.

Now let's say you made another list right next to it, of all the times you felt defeated, where you didn't show up fully, second-guessed yourself, let fear or doubt take over and as a result, you didn't achieve what you know you could have.

Then you took the same scoring system as you created above, and ranked each one of those experiences from 1-10, except this time the rating system would be in the negatives since these would be negatively impacting people (which includes you). You'd have a score of 1 representing the least amount of negative impact made on humans because of your choice and a score of 10 being the maximum amount of negative impact made on humans because of your choice.

Even if you're a pessimist and could remember more negatives than positives, I'm willing to bet that since you're not the leader of a country, the majority of occasions where you *didn't* show up fully would most usually only have a negative impact on *you*. And if that were true, you wouldn't be able to score many of those experiences higher than a 2 or 3.

Meanwhile, since humans tend to attach a higher value to experiences where we've done well for others more than the experiences where we've achieved something for ourselves, I would guess that your weighted score from this category would likely rank around 5 or above. When you make a choice that benefits other people, those people might inspire others when they tell their friends what you did. Maybe they show up more powerfully for themselves and make even better choices. This is how even one of your small acts of powerful leadership can benefit people you may not ever meet.

If I'm gonna have any hope of remembering a system, I always need some visual aids, so if you're like me, then the example below was made for you. It's made even more especially for you if you grapple with how you view your past actions and what those experiences might mean about your character or impact in this world. I want to help you see the more true, and healthier perspective on the power you've had all along.

The example below illustrates what it can look like to take inventory of the times you showed up powerfully versus the ones you *wish* you had. In the end, the exercise leads you to the conclusion that your stories of power will far outweigh any stories of smallness.

Whether you've considered yourself a leader yet or not, I'm telling you that you *are*. If you ever grapple with identifying as a leader, I'm giving you permission (not that you ever need it) to set fire to the story you've told yourself about why you're not a leader. It simply isn't true.

Whether you're a stay-at-home mom, a C-suite executive, a factory worker, a part-time freelancer, a doctor, a business owner, a retired professional, or disabled in a way that makes it difficult to work...

You.

Are.

A.

Leader.

And people notice.

Now's a good time to take a look in the Power Method Bonus Tools workbook to see how you can reinvigorate your perception on just how much you've already contributed to this world.

Go ahead, scan it, you know you want to...

Scan Me!

CHAPTER 7

CUSTOM DESIGNING YOUR LEADERSHIP STYLE

I know you've had some <u>bosses</u>, *am I right?*

Most people I know have more horror story-bosses in their work history than they do fairytale-bosses. I'm raising my hand on that one too.

Most of us cut our teeth on boss experience around the early teenage years.

A pretty common scenario might look like this:

There's a human in your workplace, let's call her Jane. You and Jane were both hired around the same time, but you didn't really love it there and you didn't try that hard, because you're 16 and you're basically just scanning documents. Jane's 19 and doesn't like to smile, she also takes her entry-level job seriously and she definitely lets you know you could be trying harder.

Cool Jane.

Anyway, the manager notices Jane's dedication and decides to offer her a managerial role. She jumps on the opportunity to make a dollar more for triple the responsibility, so Jane's moving up. And she's moving up with whatever personality, communication style, and level of emotional intelligence she had when she came in. She's the exact same person she was yesterday, except now she's in charge of you and the rest of the crew she used to share a cubicle with. This should be fun.

Jane seems like she'd fall into the "Autocratic" style of leadership, it happens to be rarely effective, but Jane doesn't know that (*and she doesn't care, okay?*).

A leadership style is the approach used by leaders to accomplish their goals. They're basically just the dominant personality styles of the boss in the workplace. There can be leaders with a blend of the approaches seen below but for the most part, one method would mostly suit us over the others, which likely speaks to our personality in general.

The leadership styles below are generally the holistic approach a leader takes in order to drive results inside their organization and among their employees, partners, and clients. These styles incorporate leadership traits. So while there are a variety of leadership styles listed below, they all have a different blend of feminine and masculine traits which combine to make them who they are.

Another way of looking at it is that the leadership traits (like the feminine traits listed previously) are like ingredients and the leadership styles (the list below) are the cake. Different ingredients create a different cake.

There are a few names for each type of leadership style that exist in the world, but the most common leadership styles that tend to get tossed around are identified as:

Affiliative: *"The people come first"* (typically effective)

Autocratic/Commanding: *"Do as I say"* (rarely effective)

Authoritative/Visionary: *"Come with me"* (commonly highly effective)

Coaching: *"Try this"* (commonly effective)

Democratic: *"What do you think?"* (typically effective)

Laissez–Faire (Hands-Off): "Hands off, let's see what you can do"(sometimes effective)

Pace–Setter: *"You've gotta keep up..."* (rarely effective)

Servant: *"How can I help"* (typically effective)

Transactional: *"Do this, get paid that"* (sometimes effective)

Transformational: *"Let's push outside the comfort zone...again"* (sometimes effective)

Another way to think of these leadership styles is imagining them as countries of origin.

For instance, let's imagine that Oprah Winfrey is from the country called "Transformational Leadership". She'd be a citizen of this country, but just like any other country, no two citizens are the same. There are similarities and values that are likely shared, but their personalities and DNA are ultimately going to be different.

What makes Oprah Winfrey such a powerful transformational leader to millions of people across the world is her ability to inspire in an authentic and personalized approach. She's emotionally tied to the stories she exposes and to the people she interviews. She chooses topics that are inherently important to most people, women especially. She's not afraid to ask difficult questions, speak her mind, and share an unpopular opinion. She owns it, all of it.

Not that we need data to support it, we see it every day, but the data is loud and clear. Positions of female leadership are not nearly as commonly held as are the positions for male leaders. And when a female, a woman of color, with even fewer career opportunities, landed a platform where millions could hear, with a message that spoke to the heart and values of women all over, she automatically inspired. She turned into a hope dealer for women all across the world, proving what's possible when women lead by example.

Oprah also models what it looks like to be a leader to other leaders, through her confidence, vulnerability, transparency, and willingness to be authentic as she comes alongside celebrities, world, and industry leaders to discuss topics of concern or global interests. She gives the guests she interviews the comfort to show up fully as themselves.

Of the leadership styles listed above, you might find one or two different styles that resonate with your personality. And if that's the case, it'd be a great opportunity to learn more about those particular styles to see which elements of each you feel the most comfortable with. Based on that, you can put your personal spin on that leadership style (or a blend of those that seem to suit you) by injecting your unique personality within it.

People ultimately want to relate to and trust a leader among them. So when a leader stands in their style but humanizes themselves enough to connect with the people they're leading, the result can be so harmonious. How you BE is another way of saying this.

Regardless of your leadership style or the environment you find yourself in, a powerful way to ignite leadership in others is by publicly applauding unique strengths. You already know how great it feels when someone acknowledges you for your effort or the results you deliver. And when they compliment you in front of others, knowing they didn't need to, but did for the sake of allowing you to shine, this boosts your confidence and loyalty to that person.

When humans get recognized for their strengths, abilities, efforts or other skills by someone in leadership, the natural tendency is to deliver even better the next time. So imagine you're part of an environment that makes this behavior part of the culture. The leaders dish out appreciation for you and your colleagues, causing you to want to out-do your last result based on the gratitude you feel for having been publicly praised. This is a healthy little back-and-forth that invites more praise and appreciation, and the cycle continues, which benefits everybody.

How would that feel for everyone involved?

So while you're looking at the various leadership styles, the most important thing to remember is that *you* are the ingredient that will make it powerful. Within the Bonus Tools Workbook you'll find an activity page that invites you to discover your own unique leadership style.

You don't exist with only a few traits, you have many, some of them might even be contradictory to one another. You might not fit into one particular leadership style either, since people are more complex than one title could ever encapsulate. And beyond that, you have a combination of a vision for yourself and your future, unlike anyone else has. This is why it can be so illuminating to discover and define how you choose to show up as the leader that you are.

Because once you can imagine a style that resonates and completely aligns with all that you're about, you can finally see yourself in it. The vision of yourself as the powerful leader in your life is the key to showing up in life as her without even having to think about it, and *that's* powerful.

So you're probably wondering where your next tool is, huh? Come on now, what kinda party do you think this is? This next bonus tool is all about helping you discover and refine the leadership style that's most powerful for you.

This is where it's going to be pretty helpful to get in the mind frame of your most confident self before going through this. This isn't the time for doubt or allowing that dialogue in your head to interrupt your flow and try to convince you that your experiences weren't that important and you don't really have much to offer.

Nope, trash that.

This is where you remember ways you've been a leader before, how that turned out for everyone, the impact it made, the confidence it gave you, and you use that as the basis for your thinking while you simultaneously imagine the most incredibly bold, powerfully, authentic, and loving version of yourself.

As you think about yourself in that light, can you *feel* her power, even just a little?

Good, now you're ready for this bonus tool because that version of you is waiting. Happy scanning!

Scan Me!

They said it...

 Jessica M.

⭐⭐⭐⭐⭐ Verified Purchase

This book will ignite your authentic self!

Reviewed in the United States on September 2, 2021

If you want to KNOW you are a leader, HOW to see yourself that way, and TRULY understand how to be your authentic self in your life and business GET THIS BOOK NOW. Sandra just knows how to help you begin connecting the dots between who you are right now and who you truly were designed to be. And then how to start connecting with others in the most genuine and powerful way. 100% a must read.

 ENY

⭐⭐⭐⭐⭐ Verified Purchase

a motivating read

Reviewed in the United States on August 29, 2021

Well written with bite-sized anecdotes that are relatable to everyday situations: It can be so easy to fall into habits that are not in our best interest, and sometimes we just need a little self-reflective push to stop settling for less.

Top reviews from United Kingdom

 S Gupta

⭐⭐⭐⭐⭐

Easy to apply and get results from all the wisdom shared

Reviewed in the United Kingdom on 31 August 2021

If you really want to get results, like true life practical results, this is a must read. Super applicable, powerful guidance and fun!

PART III | POWERFUL WORK-LIFE INTEGRATION

bal·ance

/ˈbaləns/

1. an even distribution of weight enabling someone or something to remain upright and steady.
2. a condition in which different elements are equal or in the correct proportions.

   -Oxford Languages

I don't believe in a balance between work and life anymore. The word "balance" implies an equal share across the board and when you look at your life, it includes so many different components. Striving for balance seems just as toxic to me as striving for perfection because neither will ever be achievable; they're both a mirage.

Instead of seeking a balance, I invite you in this chapter to explore the concept of work-life integration as an approach that has brought me so much relief and joy. It's a synergistic approach that enables you to allow the appropriate amount of time and energy to the diverse areas of focus in your life.

If society claims, for example, that health and well-being come first, followed by family, community, and work, then it would make sense that certain categories would require more resources depending on their rank of importance. You get to design a more joyful and on-purpose life by deciding how and when the values and responsibilities fit inside.

I'm hoping by the end of this section, you'll have been able to take a deep breath, a sigh of relief, and unlock at least one way to make your life a little easier. Let's do the dang thing.

CHAPTER 8

YOU...BETTA....WURK!

I remember growing up and hearing stories about both of my grandfathers and how they'd worked in steel factories, sometimes having two or three jobs at a time. Both sides of the family came from blue-collar roots and had a lot of pride attached to how far they'd come in life. These types of conversations were usually followed up with a reference to how much they were willing to sacrifice for their family and what great men they were because of it.

I heard about how my grandpa would get calls in the middle of the night from managers on shift at the steel plant who needed his help. So he'd get up with his eyes half-open, take the call in the kitchen while trapping himself in those old 11-foot long telephone cords as he worked on calculations to help the night manager meet his production goals. He'd completed his one-room schoolhouse education, found work, married my grandma, and had 4 amazing kids. Their life was simple but happy and this is what success looked like.

I would listen intently every time I heard a story about how my other grandpa would head off to drive one of those enormous farming tow trucks around, then clock out and round out his day with a night shift at the steel factory. He had a third-grade education and a very difficult life growing up without a father and suffering that no child should have to go through. So marrying my grandmother, raising, clothing, and feeding his four children was also a great success.

The formula was simple:

Hard Work + Financial Sacrifice = Success

Got it. Shouldn't be a problem (although I was never really keen on the sacrifice part), especially since I saw it modeled in my home growing up.

I had a stay-at-home mom who raised me and my three siblings (and no, not *everyone* in our family has four kids...oh wait, I have four kids too...). All four of us played sports competitively year-round so she was a full-time taxi, chef, housekeeper, pet caretaker, and errand-runner.

Meanwhile, my dad was an international business executive growing up. He grew up on a farm, skipped two grades in school but never got his high school diploma. He trained to become a Ferrier (think blacksmith for horseshoes), competed in the rodeo, and through his horse-shoeing work, networked his way into employment for a huge gaming company. He climbed rank in that company becoming an Executive Vice President of one of their largest divisions.

So I really did get it. The evidence was all around my family and these were people I loved, admired, and respected. If that was the only approach they talked about, and that was the only approach anyone took, then my younger brain believed it had to be the only way.

After I graduated from university, my family scattered. We all went to school in a different country or state, and my parents divorced around the same time. I met new people with new ideas, different backgrounds, and different aspirations than the ones I was used to. This offered a lot of new perspectives and appreciations, one of which included challenging the industrial mindset around the Hard Work + Sacrifice = Financial Success formula.

The ideas were conflicting directly with who I was raised to be and what it cost for my parents and grandparents to create a life they could be proud of. They made it seem like maybe my family members weren't as wise as I thought. Maybe they'd been suckered into thinking the sacrifice and *hard* work was required, just like all the other mainstream families had thought. And if that were true, that would mean my family could have done it a better way and I didn't want to think about my sweet, sacrificing grandparents with even an ounce of pity.

The ideas that provoked me were in direct conflict with the ideas I'd known. Here are some examples:

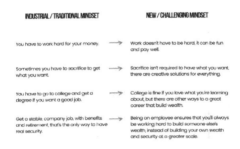

INDUSTRIAL / TRADITIONAL MINDSET		NEW / CHALLENGING MINDSET
You have to work hard for your money.	---->	Work doesn't have to be hard, it can be fun and pay well.
Sometimes you have to sacrifice to get what you want.	---->	Sacrifice isn't required to have what you want, there are creative solutions for everything.
You have to go to college and get a degree if you want a good job.	---->	College is fine if you love what you're learning about, but there are other ways to a great career that build wealth.
Get a stable, company job, with benefits and retirement, that's the only way to have real security.	---->	Being an employee ensures that you'll always be working hard to build someone else's wealth, instead of building your own wealth and security at a greater scale.

So every time I met someone or read something that challenged my way of thinking on this mindset, I looked for evidence to disprove these new opposing ideas. But what if they were right...

My grandparents were smart, and they worked very hard, but they never earned more than a blue-collar wage. So if it were ultimately true that Hard Work + Sacrifice = Financial Success, then how come the hardest people I knew weren't living in mansions?

The more I tried to disprove this new mindset around hard work, the more I found people experiencing life with extra ease, joy, passion, and wealth. I'd met women who were working less and making more. Women who never went to college, yet earned incredible money, hired out domestic services, and felt zero guilt for any of it.

I felt like I'd been kept in the dark my whole life. There were actually people in the world living like this? Don't they know they're not supposed to be able to enjoy their wealth unless they can prove they've sacrificed and worked harder than other people?

The hard-work paradigm was beginning to shift for me, and once I witnessed enough people living this way, I started to believe it could be possible in my life too. Little by little I'd start indulging in luxuries like having my groceries delivered, having meals made and delivered on certain days, working fewer hours during the week, and escalating to having vacations throughout the year *GASP!*.

And guess what happened next?

The exact opposite of what I'd expected; instead of losing money, like I thought I might from working less and investing in making life easier.

I had more energy. Here's how it worked:

I didn't have to think about which ingredients I had to shop for or how much I'd need of anything to make dinner, which always drained my energy and tanked my attitude.

It was so exciting to have extra hours in my day that I didn't want to waste them, so I'd make the most of them by doing something I loved.

I was refreshed and relaxed on vacations, giving me more energy to make progress on my priority projects when I got back.

Alternatively, I looked so forward to the vacations I'd planned, it gave me more joy and energy on the weeks leading up to the vacation.

It felt easier, with so much less resistance that I woke up happier and procrastinated less.

I had more time. Here's how it worked:

I stopped driving to the store and shopping myself, buying back about 3 hours a week.

I stopped prepping dinners and earned myself another 4-5 hours a week.

I cut 5 hours out of my day, forcing me to focus on necessities in my business only, and I found out I never needed to be doing so much of what I'd spent my time on while at my desk.

I had more money. Here's how it worked:

I saved money on gas from driving around, minimal, I admit.

Since I had more energy and time, my cognitive function was sharper and my focus was on the money-making activities in my business, rather than wasting time with busy work due to burnout.

Due to the vacations I took, I was refreshed and relaxed which sparked my creativity and ideas that led to amazing business concepts or partnership opportunities.

I felt more confident in the integration process of life and work that I said "yes" to partnership opportunities I'd run from before.

There really was something to this concept of "it gets to be easier". There are so many things we can do to enjoy our work without subscribing to the hustle & grind culture. Working to exhaustion is a way of life for a lot of people, but it's still just a perspective and a choice. It's *a* way to do things, but not the only way, and it's certainly not *my* way anymore.

It's a choice to accept the pressure from others to "grind it out" and prove you're harder working than the next person, but for what? Who does that serve? You end up exhausted, defeated, feeling like you can never keep up no matter how hard you try. And you find yourself feeling the need to beat your next hard-working performance until you have a breakdown.

The alternative is that you get to make the choice to create more joy in your day by designing a flow that allows you to get done what needs to get done, and nothing more. You set your priorities without the influence of others because this is *your* life and you're smart enough to know how to take care of yourself and others. So you can ditch the feeling of shame about working fewer hours and having more fun. That peace, energy, and focus is the rocket fuel that fuels a powerful and purposeful life.

When I was implementing this approach into my life I was concerned about how others might view my new normal. It's easy to imagine people might feel envious of this new, more relaxed, and successful version of you, but envy is not typically what comes out. More often than not, the people around you are proud of you for creating a healthier life where you're not so stressed all the time. They love you and it's likely been hard for them to watch you spin all the plates without rest like you've been doing for years. Leading yourself into a healthier shift for the sake of your sanity and joy, your family's well-being, and the success of your business or performance at work is an inspiration to the people around you.

Faith can be hard sometimes, so it's common to look for evidence that it's possible for you too. You get to successfully manage work, life, and family without being burnt out. That era is dying quickly. You don't need to be the last to shift gears and walk in a new paradigm about how you get to do life on your terms. Your life is allowed to be easier and you can get things done in a way that feels good, dare I say, even _fun?_

When you look at your average week, you can do an audit of all the activities and tasks you have during the waking hours of your day. And when you do, you can see how much time it's taking you to complete those things. When you sit with each of those items you listed and decide whether those activities, tasks, and responsibilities are increasing or decreasing your energy, you get to make a choice. Do I keep these things on my plate, can I hire them out, or can I get rid of them completely? Oh, and it might need to be said that you get to ditch _people_ too. Energy vampires can ruin your day, poison your attitude, and steal your happiness so do with this information what you will.

Practical examples help me put things into motion for myself, but as I mentioned, I'm visual and I usually need some tools to coax me along.

If you look at the example below, I show you how I've sifted through my week to identify areas that could be improved so I could have a simpler and more joyful work-life integration. There is a blank version available for you in the workbook provided through so you can make progress with this as soon as you're ready.

It's not them, its YOU.

We've got movies and television shows from as young as we can remember watching, showing us fantasies of what the perfect life can look like. A bangin' job, incredibly well-behaved kids, a brilliant and gorgeous partner who dotes on you, and friends that are nothing but fun and supportive.

These images and stories are baked into our subconscious so unless we've done the inner work to ground ourselves in reality, the knee-jerk reaction is a disappointment when our life doesn't look like that.

But perfect isn't real and neither are these on-screen fantasies. I love me some feel-good movies and a solid plotline with a powerhouse heroine, but as I evolve I try to take only the feeling of empowerment from those storylines and ditch the illusion of a life that's better than mine.

If you never watched *MADtv*, from the 90s, you missed out on a killer series called, "Lowered Expectations". It was a sketch about a dating service where everyone drops their ideals for a perfect someone and lowered their expectations to basically rock-bottom. Obviously it was exaggerated in the most amazing way, but the foundations of it are actually a pretty valuable lesson.

It's the unrealistic expectations that lead to the comparison of your life or situation to someone else's, even if they're a fictitious character. Comparison always robs us of joy, leaving us ungrateful for what we have and eliminating perspective on how far we've come. Even when we feel like we're doing better than whoever we're comparing to, that sets the standard that we need to look to someone else to decide if we're doing well in life or not. It's toxic either way.

Motherhood is an area where expectations have made me feel pretty horrible too. When I reach back into my parenting memories when I reacted in a way that I'm not proud of, it's usually because my reaction was disproportionate to the situation and not in a good way. This almost always happens if I've had unrealistic expectations coming into something.

Unreasonable expectations have a way of poisoning our environment and our mental health. We're inside our head making plans, designing our best-case scenarios and when they feel good, we get a little attached. So when we walk into the situation we've been mapping out in our heads and it doesn't materialize like that, we're disappointed. When we get disappointed, we react, and if we've had a bad day, that reaction can look pretty awful sometimes.

I was on my way home from work while I was living that corporate life years ago, and I'd had a good day at work. I had more energy than usual, plus it was a Thursday, my favorite day of the week, and the kids were off school the next day. I decided I was going to swing by our favorite pizza place and grab one of those monster-sized New York city style pizzas, get the family room set up for a movie night with a floor fort for all the kids, put on the new movie I just downloaded for them, and that I'd make popcorn and we could have the coziest night ever.

I grabbed the pizza, pulled into my driveway, ready to be the hero and I walked into the house where one kid was crying and another one was storming off because they'd been wrestling and bumped into the table, my father in law had made dinner for us and as a surprise brought it over, I'd forgotten that one of the kids had gone to a friend's house to sleepover, and my husband was exhausted from his day and wanted to go to bed early.

This is the part where Hollywood would zoom in super close to the mom standing at the door, with the huge pizza in hand, purse strapped over her shoulder, and a completely disillusioned look on her face while she stared at the chaos and watched her perfect evening fade into vapor.

I let my aggravation at this most unpleasant welcome home get the better of me and my attitude was prickly for the rest of the night.

But no one in my family even knew about my plans. I hadn't told a single one of them about my cool idea and my pizza surprise, not to mention the fact that it was lost on me until later that my awesome father in law had taken the time to cook a great meal for us and driven it to our house, just to try and make our night a little easier.

This one was on me. It was a build-up of situations like this where I realized it was my expectations that were killing the vibe. I *know* everyone feels it when I'm not happy and I don't even have to say anything at all. I didn't want to create a habit of being the mom that made you walk on eggshells because she didn't communicate her expectations or know how to control her emotional reaction when things didn't go her way. I needed to do better to model this for my kids, to keep a more peaceful home, and to maintain as much sanity for myself as I could.

I fell into a model of questioning myself with the expectations I created and it helped me calibrate to a much healthier place. I still go back to this when I feel myself start to slip, especially when it comes to remembering who's in control. For me, the faith piece is an anchor that's ultimately where I place my values and although that part might not feel true for you, that's ok. If any piece of the approach doesn't align with how you live your life, feel free to take what works for you and let the rest go:

Gauge Expectations - are they reasonable? Have they been communicated? Does it work for everyone and not just me?

Identify the Void - What need am I trying to fill by creating this expectation? What am I trying to feel from this outcome? Can I believe that I'm enough, even if this doesn't work out?

Anticipate Reality - What's the most likely outcome that might happen here? If it goes well, but not as I expect, can I be ok with that?

Remember Who's in Control - No matter how much I do, there is so much I can never control. I believe God's "got it" no matter what, so I'm going to do a better job of acting like it and living it out. This is always where I find my peace.

There's a section in the workbook to help you write these out for yourself with your next expectation. It's an exercise you might need guidance on for a bit until it becomes second nature to ask yourself the right questions.

Until then, you can access this exercise and make it your own by scanning the heck outta this:

CHAPTER 9

YOUR BRILLIANT BOUNDARIES

That was the last time.

I'd left a friend's house, who I'd been friends with for decades. I loved hanging out with her because she was hilarious and always lifted my spirits, but I was so tense on my way home that day because of how she'd been acting, *again*.

Every time I got together with her, if there were other people in the mix, she was gossiping about people she knew non-stop.

I'd tried countless times before to diffuse the conversation and steer things to a more productive place, but it was never enough to stop her behavior.

I know I don't have control over anyone else so I knew at this point I could only do two things; deal with it or give her an opportunity to improve her behavior. I also had to decide that if she wasn't willing to adjust her destructive behavior, the control I *did* have was to make the choice to stop being available for hangouts with her toxic behavior that never seemed to improve.

Before I left that day, I decided to speak up and let her know how I felt about all of it and she became really defensive, refusing to appreciate how uncomfortable it was for me and some of our other friends to tolerate.

So I told her it was probably best if we stayed friends from afar. I said goodbye and drove myself home. Over the next couple of months she'd asked two or three times if I wanted to get together with her and some of the regulars, which was when I had to remind her that it's just not for me anymore.

Since I was respectful in how I left things with her, and because the cost of hanging out with her was too expensive for my emotional well being, I didn't lose a single moment of sleep over the end of that friendship and I never hung out with her again after that. I love her as a person but I choose not to surround myself with the negative that gets ejected when conversations run wild.

And you know what? I feel *amazing* knowing that I don't have people in my life that speak about others in those ways. I don't even think about it anymore. I don't have to carefully navigate speech or try to convince people to be less hurtful, it's so much more peaceful.

When you ignore your boundaries, you might not realize that you can easily get taken advantage of. But if you go back and think about the times you've felt as though you *were* being taken advantage of, think about whether or not you had clear boundaries with the person involved in that scenario.

Without the self-respect that comes from implementing and enforcing your boundaries, people end up taking more than they need (and possibly more than you have) in the form of time, money, respect, and other precious resources that can cost you more than you're ready for.

The harsh part here is that you're letting them do that. When an area of your life has fuzzy boundaries or none at all, you're allowing people to ransack the place. Not everyone will do that to you but the human nature side will take over for the people that aren't as aware of their behavior patterns when it comes to respecting other people.

What can end up happening after a while is that you won't respect yourself as a person. You'll have less confidence and you'll probably stop trusting yourself as much. It's just not possible to thrive while you're living in a state where your confidence is diminished and you're convinced that everyone else's needs come before your own.

Whether you own your own business, work for an employer, or stay at home, you want success but I know you're not trying to work so much that you'll never see your family. I'm certain you're not trying to burn yourself out and develop dangerous stress-induced health complications. And I'm sure you don't want to lose sight of what really matters to you in life and become one of those people that chases money as if that's the thing that ultimately defines your worth.

At some point along the way, family, peers, culture, and media all have an influence on what we think we need in order to view ourselves as successful. When we don't obtain these things, it gets real easy to believe we're not worth anything if we don't have them. Because hey, society says you're great if you've got 'em, so what's wrong with you if you don't?

But your worth was never defined by any material things. It's not defined by what you accomplish or the title you carry. Your worth isn't determined by what you *haven't* accomplished either. You've been worthy all along because you were born that way.

When it comes to your health, family, work, relationships, finances, and technology, creating boundaries becomes incredibly empowering. So designing them in a way that suits your values and goals enables you to start living a life that feels more aligned, gives you more energy, earns you more money, and delivers more peace will be critical to master.

That might sound like a lot of work, but trust me, these things can all be managed so well with baby steps. You shouldn't tackle all the categories at once. Instead, you can handle them one at a time, using small shifts.

For instance, boundaries related to finance, you might consider how much money from each paycheck you vow to save. Decide what your monthly ceiling of spending is for going out to eat. You can set a standard for how much money you'll put toward credit card repayment every month and whether you do that weekly or biweekly(which matters if you carry a large balance to save more on interest).

You can decide that you'll never spend more than a certain number of dollars on miscellaneous items on vacation, or that you'll always give at least $50 per month to your favorite charitable cause with intentions to grow to a certain number you have in mind. The idea is to strike a healthy balance for your financial boundaries by marrying something that's both comfortable to you and also gets you in a stronger financial position.

The same goes for relationships. If you aren't currently in a relationship with someone else, you can create boundaries around the type of partner you're willing to date. Alternatively, you'll want to supplement those boundaries by identifying the type of partner that you envision as the best fit for you while keeping in mind the type of traits you'll *never* be ok with in a partner (I'm willing to bet you have a few life lessons that can help guide you here). This particular boundary falls under the personal and professional categories for two reasons.

Firstly, having a healthy romantic relationship with someone will only strengthen your ability to show up and do your job better, while a toxic or draining relationship will pull you out of focus, rob you of energy and passion, and stunt your creativity in your work and social life.

The second way this is relevant in work and business is that you might be on the verge of inviting a partner into a business relationship with you. In this case, it's incredibly important for the state of your business that you decide which types of character traits and moral values you'll feel comfortable working side-by-side with. If you have to show up every day to work on and in a business with someone who doesn't share your outlook, values, or commitment to quality, stress and resentment will slowly start to break down the business itself.

Integrity is a big one. Integrity is defined by the reputation of honesty and having strong moral character and judgment. If you're reading this book at all, it tells me you actually care about becoming a better version of yourself so integrity is likely a value that's near the top of your list. You've got people in your social circle, including your family, who look to you with an amount of trust. The measure of how much trust you're able to receive from someone comes from the type of integrity you carry around with you.

When your behaviors are in line with the integrity you claim to have, your trust factor with others increases. If you're known by others as someone who does what they say they'll do and means it when they say, "No", your relationships become stronger and your experiences with people get richer.

Some boundaries you can create around integrity are rules surrounding truth. Deciding to commit to telling the truth, regardless of how scary it might be to deliver the information. It never feels good when you know you've let someone down and you're about to tell them what happened, or inform a team member that a deal is going south, or that you've lost feelings for someone and don't want to pretend anymore. But deciding to tell the truth and be upfront with them, no matter what benefits your soul. You go to bed at night with peace, knowing you did your best, trusted your intuition, and respected that person enough to tell them the truth no matter how uncomfortable it was for both of you.

They'll eventually get over the bad news you brought, but they'll always remember that you honored them enough to tell them the truth. Think about the last time you were on the other side of this type of interaction, where someone told you a difficult truth out of respect for you and it stung. After your emotions settled, did you appreciate the direct approach? Did you consider whether or not you would have had the guts to say it if the shoe were on the other foot? When we stand in integrity, we mark another occasion where we choose to be powerful in the moment, setting an example for others as a leader and inviting them to challenge them to assess their own character in the same regard.

When it comes to technology, this is a huge interrupter within the family nucleus these days. Parents walking around with cell phones glued to their faces while their toddlers act out for attention and quality time. Eventually, those toddlers grow up a little less connected, get phones of their own, and model exactly what they watched their parents do while they were growing up. When I was young, the only real technology anyone was concerned about having too much of was t.v., since there weren't cell phones or internet yet. But since our tech has evolved and become entirely mobile, we have access to everything no matter where we are so the habits become more destructive to the family unit and our own mental health.

Creating your own rules around the tech in your home regarding when and where technology is allowed can become so liberating to everyone in the house. For instance, a few of the boundaries we've placed around tech in our home is that no one in my family is allowed to bring their phone to the table. Phones aren't allowed in the bedroom at night, and neither are computers. Our dinners are more fun, the kids get better sleep, the temptations and dangers of the internet are decreased since nothing good happens with kids after 10 pm anyway.

Every family is different so it's important to decide what you're willing to be ok with and if you have a partner and kids in your life, deciding together what's the fairest and most sensible for your family is the path of least resistance to ensuring cooperation for the approach you're trying on. You can even set a time limit and decide that you'll try your new boundaries out for a month and see how everyone feels, allowing you to adjust and create boundaries that suit you best.

At first, boundaries always feel like restrictions, whether you're a child or an adult. But as you get good with the idea that this is what you've committed to and there's no negotiating with your kids, your partner, and you will start to appreciate the time where no one's distracted by things that matter much less than family.

I've included an exercise to help you customize your boundaries in all the areas I mentioned above. Most people have never written their boundaries down, instead of going with their gut for decisions as they happen. But when you have guidelines to what you're willing to accept and what you're not, less confusion, chaos, stress, and discomfort occur in your life. While the joy, freedom, connections, respect, and wealth can increase to measures you've never experienced before.

CHAPTER 10

TIME'S UP

I sat down at my desk, popped open my laptop, clicked on my zoom link, and waited for my client to join. Her face popped up and I smiled hugely and greeted her with the obnoxious, *"HAAAAAAAAAAAY!"* that always makes her laugh. She wasn't laughing though. Her eyes were red and her messy bun was falling to the side of her head and she didn't have to say a word for me to know she was having one heckuva day.

"HOW DO YOU DO IT?! How do you have twice the amount of kids I do, another business, travel, and you're making it all happen? I can't find time for the things I need and want to do and I feel like I'm falling apart!"

Not how I expected us to start, since she was usually super up-beat. So it was assessment time. I needed more information on what was going on in her life, what her typical day looked like, and which areas seemed to be spiraling so I could try and help.

She was in a system of responding and reacting. Her days were getting away from her by the time her coffee was ready in the morning and she'd get interrupted with other people's priorities throughout the day. After listening to everything in detail, I knew she needed two things; boundaries work and a time management boot camp.

A little over a week later, as I sat at my desk cautious to join our zoom link this time, she joined with a big fat smile on her face (and the bun was in the right spot). She'd implemented almost everything we talked about and she was getting more done in less time and was more excited to show up for her business than she'd been in a long time.

This type of progress comes from alignment and purpose in a way that's even more powerful than motivation; it's momentum and it's self-generated.

The method I use and one of the most successful methods I teach my clients are to build their day around their energy levels, not their time. We all have a certain cycle of energy throughout the day with some people thriving with energy and focus early in the morning while others can't do single-digit addition till nearly lunchtime (*cough* raises hand).

There are loads of books and practices telling everyone they have to get up at 4 or 5 am if they want to have a thriving business or a healthier life. But trying to get people who naturally lack energy and focus to get up and do heavy mental lifting on projects or tasks before the sun comes up will only ensure those projects look like hot trash on fire.

Instead, you can identify the natural energy levels you have throughout the day and leverage the high energy, high-focus times to work on things that require more creativity or a higher level of attention to detail. I have a worksheet I use for this but you can even do this by color-coding your digital calendar in energy blocks.

An easy way to start is by blocking off time for family and sleep as the first and most obvious block of time. You know when you sleep so those hours are off the table, and you know when you're typically spending time with family so if you block that off in its own separate color, you can make sure to see it and protect it.

Once that's off the table, you're left with the middle chunk of your day, a pretty big portion. Using a separate color to block off the time in the day where you have the most energy allows you to see exactly when you should be spending time on the mentally intensive activities to boost your productivity and efficiency.

Any windows of time outside of that can be color-coded for more low-key items that don't require much of a mental lift. For me, that's gonna be morning, *for sure.* I can't get crankin' til at least 11 am so I spend the morning doing things that don't take much effort.

Things like:

- Audio trainings if I have them
- Podcast episodes
- Updating notes or feedback for team members
- Chores
- Errands
- Light admin tasks, etc.

And when that power hour/flow time starts to hit, you can be ready to take on things that require your brain power like:

- Creative tasks

- Book writing
- Client trainings
- Project management
- Designing
- Planning, etc.

So at the end of the day, I've gotten done as much as I'm able to, feeling satisfied, purposeful, and proud. My family knows my schedule and they understand why I do what I do and when my brain is best suited for big conversations.

When you can see your week color-coded in this way, it's visual evidence of where you're putting your priorities. So if what you see doesn't feel good, you get to decide which colors need to be bigger, and where.

You can check out the scheduling tool I've included inside your Bonus Tools workbook so you can craft an easier week for yourself.

UGH! I'm tellin' ya, when you start applying this approach it can be so incredibly energizing and joy-inducing, so fair warning; you might smile a lot more. I said what I said.

But nothing's perfect because life happens, and things come up, even for small seasons where it's not ideal. That's when you pivot for the priorities, do your best, and get back to your time management system as soon as life allows.

YOUR POWER IS WAITING.

It is my hope that by seeing yourself as you were created to be seen, with more power than you can imagine, more potential for greatness, and the embodiment of a leader that people truly need, you'll be able to take steps into the version of yourself that's waiting just around the corner.

And if that version of yourself is as powerful as I know she is, she's the woman who respects herself and the ones she loves, enough to create brilliant boundaries that feel liberating and energizing, while she lives her days honoring her natural energy levels to get more done than ever before.

Your life is so important. You have so many unique gifts and experiences to share and bless people around you with. The people in your life are so much better for having you around and it's not because of anything you've done, it's simply because you're you. You are worth every single dream, desire, and vision you have for yourself so not only can you have it, you deserve it.

I hope this book has served you in some way and if you'd like to connect in more ways than this book, this link will take you to the places I hang out and you can decide which platform is right for you. If you're not a social media person, mad respect, and I've still gotchu...

You can reach out by email to
powermethod@sandrahaseley.com

Or scan your heart out with this lil' cutie pie.

Stay awesome and remember to always *#GOBIGGER.*

OH, AND ONE MORE THING...

What, you thought that was it?

I'm girl-gang for life, and since I knew a book could only do so much, I created the workbook to go along with this.

But you might need more than that to keep your momentum flying.

If you own your own business and you need support, whether it's the accountability and strategies or the mentorship and guidance along the way, you're invited to reach out. While I do only have a small number of one-on-one coaching spots available each month, I've got ways that make it easy for you to work with me in different containers.

And for the women who are dying to vibe on all things powerful, inspired, and growth-oriented, I've got experiences for you that you're not gonna wanna miss.

Either way, I'm so glad this book found it's way to you on purpose and I know there are great things ahead for you.

OTHER WAYS TO CONNECT:

I'm not everywhere all the time, but I'll check in on all of the places listed. In terms of where I *usually* spend more time, in order of rank:

Instagram, Facebook, TikTok, LinkedIn (and who just hangs out on their website? My team is definitely actively responding to anything website related so all of the places listed are good to go.

But I love making your life easier, so you can just scan this **one** little cutie pie of a QR code to get to all of my channels at once...like magic...

scan for ALL the things

POWER-PACKED SPONSORS

On the next few pages, I'm featuring some INCREDIBLE women that I want you to check out and get to know.

These women are walking the talk in their communities and building up women everywhere they go. They serve hard, leading with love, they listen with compassion and empathy, but they fiercely stand in who they are and defend the smaller voices among them.

These women are heroes to more than just me. And they've done something incredible with this book. They sponsored books in order to get more copies into the hands of women who need to be reunited with everything that makes them so amazing. My hope is that they, along with all the women who read this book, are better off for having done it.

Please take a moment to visit these women online, connect with them and support them in any way that feels aligned to you.

And to my incredible sponsors, cheers to *YOU,* and those big, beautiful, brave hearts of yours.

MAVEN LEVEL SPONSORSHIP:

TRICIA SNYDER

The owner of TRISH, a boutique with chic, classic pieces where women are empowered to discover their unique style.

With over 30 years experience in the fashion business from LA to NY and store locations formerly in Aspen and now back to her hometown in Virginia , TRISH brings style and confidence to her discerning clients.

Her constant go to for fashion foundation is to "KEEP IT CLASSY", by creating style aligned for each of her clients' unique values and lifestyle so they feel empowered, confident, and beautiful.

Retail therapy is an experience inside this gorgeous boutique with an intentional commitment to being overly honest with our clients in order to remain the level of trust we've earned from them. Our online clients get the same attention while experiencing our boutique through a high-touch virtual approach.

TRISH has the ability to transform your fantasy style into a reality wardrobe that will never be complicated but always complemented.

Her secret life may just be finding some pages to BLOW UP in a new book soon. It's a responsibility to help others not go through the same mistakes when you have been there and done that.

(SCAN ME!)

SILENT SPONSOR

This particular woman wishes to remain unknown as she'd rather not have the light shine on her. This is so typical of the powerful, generous, loving,

compassionate and driven Maven behind this sponsorship. She's a mother and brilliant woman who leads her global company in excellence, inspires her hundreds of employees, and serves her community with a continued legacy of her family's philanthropy. I believe I can speak on behalf of all women when I say we are all better off for having you lead the way you do.

Thank you, sincerely.

MOXIE LEVEL SPONSORSHIP:

IRENE ELBIE

The brilliant editor behind The Power Method and a dear friend of Sandra's, Irene is proud to serve through the "Strength Beside the Badge". Irene makes it her mission to come along side spouses of first responders to teach them how to find their strength and compassion while reconnecting with love and faith, unapologetically.

She has an enormous heart and is fiercely loyal to everyone who counts on her. She is absolutely a woman you want to connect with.

BOOK A FREE CONSULTATION WITH IRENE:

ANDREA COSTRINO

The photographer responsible for the cover art photos on this book and one of Sandra's closest friends. She's the owner of Andrea Costrino & Co., a Buffalo, NY-based  photography studio specializing in legacy portraits for women who desire to feel empowered and confident in their own skin.

In the safe space of her studio, Andrea provides a one-of-a-kind experience with her clients that allows them to feel seen and heard, while gently guiding them to step out of their comfort zone in order to produce portraits that her clients are proud of.

Connect with Andrea using this QR code:

ACKNOWLEDGEMENTS

I wouldn't be here without the help, support, inspiration, love, friendship, kindness, comic relief, and listening skills of these unbelievable women. Thank you for being there and thank you for everything you are.

Patti Lister – Thank you for creating me, loving me, teaching me, and believing in me. You taught me the foundations of power, leadership, and work-life integration as I know it. You also made it all fun and still make me laugh m'arse off.

Shiran Cohen – The Power Method wouldn't have looked this way without you, you are WOVEN into the pages. The kindness, generosity, love, and support you've extended is other-wordly. No one knows a friend like you. Soul magic. NESHAMA SHELLY.

Andrea Costrino – For taking the photos that appear on the front and back of this book along with all the other incredible creations. You are an artist. Thank you for seeing the future version of me and making me look and feel more powerful with everything you do.

Irene Elbie – For being a heartbeat into the message behind this book, for your editing skeelz, and your incredible encouragement and love. Your heart and willingness to love fully will always be an inspiration to me.

Maria Violante - You've been the classy, cool, brilliant, strong woman all along. You're as real as they come and you've always been such a safe place for me. Keep inspiring everyone around you and I'll keep fan-girling your biceps.

Amber Beyer – You walk by example with everything you do. Your resilience, authenticity, fun, and outpouring of generosity to the people in the entire community is nothing short of awe-inspiring. Thank you for setting the bar as high as you have for women everywhere to believe they're capable of so much more. You trend-setting jack of all trades powerhouse, you.

AND To my "league of legends" who blessed this book to go out into the world...

Shiran Cohen, Andrea Costrino, Irene Elbie, Maria Violante, Julie Kirkland, Casie Zarin, Vanessa Napolitano Duarte, Tricia Snyder, Lynnette LaRoche, Tricia Fraley, Kelsey Knutson, Jennie Rae Oates, Jessica Madrigal, Tonya Davis, Rachael Edmondson-Clarke, Laura Brunton, Nicki Young, Bogi Kom, Avion

Hercules, Marah Förster, Sumeena Gupta, Milda Sabiene, Tanya McCreedy, Jennifer Brown, Vera Mernacaj, Sarah Lux, Rosetta Enrica Matina, Eva Kaszycki.

This book wouldn't have felt right without your eyes, hearts, and minds on this. I love you and I'm so grateful for each one of you.

ABOUT THE AUTHOR

Sandra Haseley is a Canadian-born American wife and mother of four amazing children who works full time as a business strategist, high-performance coach, international best-selling author, and keynote speaker, passionate about guiding fearless and high-vibe women who are ready for breakthroughs into a simpler, more joyful, and wealthier next levels. And she really likes snacks.

She is the owner of Sandra Haseley + CO. and founding partner of Generation Impact Consulting, LLC., working with thousands of women from all across the world. She teaches them how to build and scale their businesses using proven strategies, tactics, and a powerful mindset while working less and having way more fun.

She has also been hired as a corporate consultant for multimillion-dollar businesses for program development, branding, speaking, and workshop creation.